★ICONS

★ICONS

JG
PRESS

Published in 2010 by
World Publications Group, Inc.
140 Laurel Street,
East Bridgewater, MA 02333
www.wrldpub.com

10 9 8 7 6 5 4 3 2 1

ISBN 978-1-57215-659-3

Authors: Judith Millidge and Jessica Hodge

Printed and manufactured in China

Contents

Introduction

What makes an icon? Icons were once religious objects of devotion, beautifully crafted, gilded representations of saints and holy people. Today, the word has come to mean someone, real or imaginary, who has come to symbolize a concept or an institution, whether it be political, religious or cultural.

All the people in this book stand out. They may have been the first, the best, or simply the most memorable person in their field, whether it is as a smoldering screen siren (Marilyn), an intrepid explorer (Sir Edmund Hillary), or the world's most famous and longest-lived cartoon character (Mickey Mouse). More than that, individually they have come to symbolize one particular aspect of their fame. Clark Gable, for example, is the archetypal Hollywood idol of the 1930s and 1940s; Michael Jordan epitomizes the winning, all-American sportsman; and Madonna is the embodiment of the high achieving rock chick. Icons not only excel in their work, they embody it and their success is so all consuming that the rest of us can only look on in awe.

Popular icons are a 20th-century innovation, made possible only by the mass media – film, television, record labels and newspapers. Earlier generations simply did not have such objects of veneration. Without the oxygen of publicity, stars cannot shine – or if they do, precious few people get to hear about them. Andy Warhol, the iconic pop artist, once said that everyone would be famous for 15 minutes, but for everyone in this book, that is a gross underestimation. Icons are not one-hit wonders, but people who prove, time and again, that they are excellent at what they do. Many a singer's career has hit the doldrums because public tastes change, but the really iconic – Cher, Tina Turner and Marvin Gaye, for example – often reinvent themselves, as times change. Others, such as David Bowie, are famous for their chameleon-like abilities to change their image; for some, like the great actor Laurence Olivier, it is this ability that helps define them.

Some icons – the Rolling Stones, Aretha Franklin, or Stevie Wonder – merit inclusion because of a longevity that enhances their stellar talents. However, other stars shine all too briefly, leaving a searing image burnt on the retinas of the world that can be replayed over and over, but never recaptured in their original glory. James Dean, Jimi Hendrix and Jim Morrison all bowed out at the height of their powers, leaving behind a memorable body of work, an eternally youthful image and a heavy cloud of nostalgia.

Selecting the list has not been easy and it is unlikely that any two people would come up with the same collection. The iconic stars in these pages share a number of qualities – undoubted talent, dedication, hard work and a bit of luck. All of them are famous for their achievements, unlike many recent celebrities who are famous simply for being famous.

True icons stand the test of time. They embody qualities that their fans want to emulate and their appeal is timeless, crossing continents and spanning generations.

Muhammad Ali

Born Cassius Marcellus Clay Jr.
January 17, 1942
Louisville, Kentucky, USA

Renowned American boxer and three times world heavyweight champion, Muhammad Ali has long been hailed as 'the Greatest'. His stunning record, unorthodox fighting style and gift of the gab have lifted him to superstar status.

Muhammad Ali (originally born, Cassisus Clay Jr.) was born in Louisville, Kentucky. His father, Cassius Marcellus Clay Sr., was named after a 19th-century Kentucky politician and anti-slavery campaigner. It was a local police officer and boxing coach who first encouraged the 12-year-old Cassius to box, when they found the boy fuming over the theft of his bicycle. As an amateur, Clay went on to win an astonishing 100 out of his 105 matches, culminating in a gold medal in the light heavyweight division at the 1960 Olympics in Rome.

After his Olympic triumph he turned professional. Perfecting his line in pre-match verbal hype, he won all 19 of his fights between 1960 and 1963, though there were some close calls. When he met world heavyweight champion, Sonny Liston, in Miami in February 1964, he was not widely tipped to win. At the weigh-in, Ali taunted Liston, famously saying that he would 'float like a butterfly, sting like a bee'. Unusually tall, at 190 cm (6 ft 3 in), he did not hold his hands high to protect his face in the accepted heavyweight style, but instead relied on speed, dexterity and his powerful jab. At 22, Ali's win against Liston made him the youngest boxer ever to take a title from a reigning heavyweight champion – in his own words, 'I shook up the world'. He shook it up some more in 1964, joining the, then controversial, Nation of Islam movement and adopting the name, Muhammad Ali. In early 1966, he responded to the Vietnam draft by declaring himself a conscientious objector. Found guilty of refusing to serve, he was stripped of his title and boxing license.

Ali appealed and the Supreme Court reversed his conviction in June 1971. He was allowed to fight again from 1970 and soon afterwards took part in three iconic bouts. He suffered his first professional loss against Joe Frazier in the hugely hyped 'Fight of the Century' on March 8, 1971. But the 'Rumble in the Jungle' in Zaire in October 1974, in one of the biggest upsets in boxing history, Ali regained his heavyweight title by outlasting and outclassing the champion, George Foreman. And in October 1975, in a final clash with Frazier billed as the 'Thrilla in Manila', he was the victor in the 15th and final round.

Ali retired in 1981, having defeated every top heavyweight of his time and was sadly diagnosed with Parkinson's disease in 1984. He has become a widely respected and loved public figure, working with the US civil rights movement and the United Nations. In 2005 he received the Presidential Medal of Freedom from President George W. Bush.

Left: Ali lands a winning punch on Floyd Patterson during their 1965 heavyweight title fight.

Below: Ali retained his fighting form until his retirement in 1981.

Woody Allen

Born Allen Stewart Konigsberg
December 1, 1935
Brooklyn, New York, USA

Actor, screenwriter, musician and playwright, the multi-talented Woody Allen is, above all, a prolific film director, who writes all his own films. He is one of the few American directors whose dominant creative role gives his many films, from romantic comedies to serious dramas, a highly distinctive style.

The only son of Orthodox Jewish parents, Allen grew up in a middle-class Brooklyn neighborhood. His devoted, quizzical relationship with New York remains one of the defining threads of his work, above all in *Manhattan* (1979), a black-and-white love song to his home city. His early film passions, never abandoned, were for the Marx Brothers and Humphrey Bogart. But his early career was as a comic – first as a contributor to radio shows and then on stage himself, as a stand-up comedian. His uniquely New York Jewish act defined the Allen persona – intellectual, insecure, neurotic and classically funny. Allen stepped into the movie world in 1965, when he was hired to write the screenplay for the sharp, farcical *What's New, Pussycat?*, in which he also had a role. Early stage work included his tribute to Bogart, *Play It Again, Sam*, which he filmed in 1972, launching his long association with his co-star, Diane Keaton.

His best-known work with Keaton, *Annie Hall* (1977), marked a move into more thoughtful and sophisticated territory, while retaining all Allen's entertaining satiric edge. It was a huge critical and box office success. Throughout his career, Allen has continued to play with different styles and techniques. Some of his less popular films of the 1970s and 1980s, such as *Interiors* (1978) and *September* (1987), showed the influence of European film directors, notably Ingmar Bergman.

His more mainstream work from this time, including the Oscar-winning *Hannah and Her Sisters* (1986) – inspired by his relationship with Mia Farrow – and *Crimes and Misdemeanors* (1989), also introduced a more serious, even tragic, tone alongside the comedy. This darker note recurs in the emotionally violent *Husbands and Wives* (1992), with its jumpy, hand-held camerawork and pessimistic view of enduring love. This was filmed during his very public break-up with Farrow.

Allen's response to personal upheaval was to revert to humor, with the comic thriller *Manhattan Murder Mystery* (1993) and the glorious period comedy *Bullets over Broadway* (1994). The latter depicted the lush theater world of the 1930s, an era which also featured in *Sweet and Lowdown* (1999). Allen continues to be prolific, but more recent work has had a mixed reception. *Match Point* (2005), the story of a social-climbing tennis pro, was an interesting development, being shot, not in Allen's beloved New York, but in London. And *Vicky Cristina Barcelona* (2008), again filmed in a new and evocative location, marked a full return to the intelligent, thoughtful, romantic comedies for which Allen is best loved.

Right: Woody Allen is one of America's most thought-provoking and interesting film directors.

Below: Allen with Diane Keaton on the set of *Annie Hall*, 1977.

Pedro Almodóvar

Born Pedro Almodóvar
Caballero
September 25, 1949
Calzada de Calatrava,
Cuidad Real, Spain

A self-taught Spanish film-maker, the openly gay Pedro Almodóvar has come a long way from his backwoods origins in provincial Spain. Acclaimed for his flamboyant plotting, melodramatic storylines and subtle and perceptive roles for women, he is regarded by many as the most inspired and prolific Spanish film-maker of his day.

Determined from childhood to make movies, Almodóvar began his career in 1960s Madrid, where the dictator, General Franco, had just closed the National School of Cinema. His first short films, made with a hand-held camera, were outrageously melodramatic and overtly sexual, in part, no doubt, a protest against an oppressive regime. His early work also shows the influence of Hollywood film noir and screwball comedy.

With Franco's death in 1975, Almodóvar became a leading light in Madrid's cultural renaissance, working with Carmen Maura, the first of several actresses with whom he established a creative partnership and the then unknown Antonio Banderas.

The sex-and-death-fixated *Matador* (1986) and the stylish and complex *Law of Desire* (1987) used extreme and shocking content to make serious points. The light comedy *Women on the Verge of a Nervous Breakdown* (1988) was Almodóvar's international breakthrough, while *High Heels* (1991) was an early example of his fascination with fractured female relationships, here between a self-involved mother and the daughter she abandoned.

A key transitional film is *The Flower of My Secret* (1995), which focuses on a neglected wife finding her own path to self-esteem. It paved the way for the trio of increasingly confident films that made Almodóvar's international reputation. *Live Flesh* (1997) saw his first collaboration with Penélope Cruz, who has since became another of his regulars, while *All About My Mother* (1999), revisiting the now familiar themes of sisterhood and family, won more awards and honors than any other Spanish film and established Almodóvar in the movie mainstream. The daring *Talk to Her* (2002), a potentially bleak tale of two men caring for women in comas, unfolds in a delicate series of flashbacks and is a moving reflection on the nature of love and devotion. It won Almodóvar an Oscar for its screenplay.

Family relationships also form the theme of the 2006 *Volver*, a tragi-comic tale of female solidarity and resilience, shot in the rural Spain of the director's childhood. It unites two of Almodóvar's best-loved muses: Carmen Maura plays a feckless mother and Penélope Cruz gives a career-best, Oscar-nominated performance as her grown-up daughter.

Broken Embraces (2009), again starring Cruz, is Almodóvar's longest and most expensive movie to date. It features a complex and opaque structure of flashback and film-within-film, which has become one of Almodóvar's signature notes.

Left: Almodóvar directing the psychological drama, *La Flor de Mi Secreto* (*The Flower of My Secret*), 1995.

Below: Almodóvar is the best known Spanish film-maker of his generation and his movies have a huge international following.

Fred Astaire

Born Frederick Austerlitz
May 10, 1899
Omaha, Nebraska, USA

Died June 22, 1987
Los Angeles, California,
USA

Debonair, charming and extraordinarily graceful, Fred Astaire was the ultimate Hollywood song-and-dance man. He revolutionized dance on camera, both as a solo dancer and paired with a succession of dancing actresses, most famously Ginger Rogers.

In his signature top hat, white tie and tails, Astaire was a popular romantic lead in the 1930s and 1940s, despite his lack of movie-star good looks. He also made some of the best-loved films of the time, from *Top Hat* with Rogers (1935) to *Silk Stockings* with Cyd Charisse (1957).

Astaire's career began at the tender age of seven, as a vaudeville partner to his older sister, Adele. The pair made it to Broadway in 1917, working with the Gershwins and starring in shows such as *Lady Be Good* (1924) and *Funny Face* (1927). Following Adele's marriage and retirement in 1932, Hollywood came calling in the form of David O. Selznick, who signed Astaire to RKO and partnered him with Ginger Rogers, in a sequence of unmatchable films which elevated both leads to stardom. Katharine Hepburn reportedly said: 'He gives her class, she gives him sex.' Astaire's light tenor married well with Rogers' breathy soprano, but it was the quality of the dancing that set their films apart. The choreography, by Astaire and Hermes Pan, introduced dance as an intrinsic element of the Hollywood film musical; six of the nine musicals Astaire created for RKO became their biggest moneymakers.

Astaire's work with later song-and-dance partners tends to get overshadowed by the glamor and nostalgia of the Astaire/Rogers years. But his movie work continued to be fresh and innovative. *Broadway Melody of 1940* featured an extended dance routine with the brilliant tap-dancer Eleanor Powell, who was Astaire's first partner after Rogers. *You'll Never Get Rich* (1941), with Rita Hayworth, allowed Astaire to introduce Latin American dance rhythms into his routines and after a brief retirement in 1946, he came storming back to make *Easter Parade* (1949) opposite Judy Garland. His co-stars in the 1950s included Jane Powell, Leslie Caron and Audrey Hepburn (*Funny Face*, 1957).

After 30 musical films in 25 years, Astaire turned in the 1960s and 1970s to a series of Emmy-winning music and dance specials made for television and to straight film. He received his only Oscar nomination, as Best Supporting Actor, for his role in *The Towering Inferno* (1974).

As a singer, Astaire introduced and left his mark on classics such as *Fascinating Rhythm*, *Foggy Day*, and *Nice Work if You Can Get It*. As a virtuoso dancer, with superb technical control and an innate sense of rhythm, he drew his influences from a wide range of sources, from tap dance to ballet to ballroom. The result was his uniquely personal 'outlaw style,' which is still influential today.

Left: Astaire and Ginger Rogers at their most glamorous, 1949. They starred together in ten films.
Right: 'I'm just a hoofer with a spare set of tails,' said Fred Astaire, whose long career lasted an incredible 76 years.

Sir David Attenborough

A naturalist, broadcaster and television pioneer, Sir David Attenborough is among the most outstanding and best-loved broadcasters of his generation. Knighted by Queen Elizabeth II in 1985, he has many other civic and academic honors to his name.

After a science degree at Cambridge and national service in the Royal Navy, Attenborough joined the BBC as a trainee in 1952, the very early days of television. His long association with natural history programs began in 1954, as the presenter of *Zoo Quest*. After leaving the BBC in the early 1960s, he was summoned back in a surprise move in 1965 as Controller of BBC2. This new channel had been launched the previous year but was struggling to find its feet.

Attenborough's clear sense of what publicly funded broadcasting should offer galvanized BBC2; he established a diverse range of programs that defined the chaannel for decades. Commissions included classics, such as the quiz show *Call My Bluff*, the self-help *Money Programme* and the revolutionary late-night contemporary music program, *The Old Grey Whistle Test*. To mark the advent of color, he commissioned a landmark and hugely successful 13-part history of western art, *Civilisation*, introduced by art historian, Kenneth Clark. This was followed by two further authored documentaries, Jacob Bronowski's *The Ascent of Man* and Alistair Cooke's *America*.

But at heart, Attenborough was a program-maker and his promotion in 1969 to Director of Programmes left him little time for filming. In 1973, he resigned to return to documentary making and writing. He had begun planning the *Life on Earth* series while still a manager and was now able to take on the role of presenter himself. His committed and serious approach to film-making engaged the interest and co-operation of the scientific community, gaining his team privileged access – who can forget Attenborough with Dian Fossey's research group of mountain gorillas? Novel film-making techniques were developed, too, to get the shots he wanted and the result is television history, with the series still retailing on DVD today.

The success of *Life on Earth* encouraged the BBC to commission a new series, *The Living Planet*, screened in 1984 and focusing on how living organisms adapt to their environment. *The Trials of Life* (1990) looked at animal behavior, causing some audience consternation with its depiction of the realities of hunter and hunted. Still on a roll, Attenborough then turned his attention to more specialized areas of the natural world, beginning with

Born David Frederick Attenborough
May 8, 1926
London, England

The Private Life of Plants (1995), which again required ingenious camerawork, as well as time-lapse techniques, to bring its subject alive. *The Life of Birds* (1998), *The Life of Mammals* (2002), *Life in the Undergrowth* (2005) and *Life in Cold Blood* (2008) all followed. The result is a consistent and encyclopaedic body of natural history programs that have become a benchmark of quality, technical innovation and intellectual rigor.

Left: The elder statesman of natural history broadcasting, Attenborough set the standard by which all others are judged.

Below: Attenborough with a llama at London Zoo in 1980, the year after his landmark series, *Life on Earth*.

Brigitte Bardot

Born Camille Javal
September 28, 1934
Paris France

Bardot was the original gorgeous, pouting European starlet of the 1950s. With her flowing blonde hair, voluptuous figure and sensuous beauty, she was a successful model and had a thriving movie career until the 1970s. Since then she has devoted much of her time to animal rights activism.

Bardot was born in Paris, the daughter of a wealthy industrialist and was a talented ballet dancer. In 1947 she began studying at the prestigious Conservatoire National Supérieur de Musique et de Danse de Paris. In 1949 she was spotted while modeling in a fashion show and in March 1950, she appeared on the cover of *Elle* magazine. Her captivating looks attracted the attention of film director, Marc Allegret, and he sent his assistant, Roger Vadim to audition her for a film role. Bardot did not immediately acquire a movie contract, but in 1952, Vadim became the first of her four husbands. Still aged only 18, Bardot made her movie debut the same year in a comedy, *Le Trou Normand* (titled *Crazy for Love* for the English-speaking market).

She made 17 films between 1952 and 1956, including small parts in three English-language movies, but Vadim felt that her talents were not being adequately showcased. Keen to show that she was a serious actor, he cast her in *And God Created Woman* in 1956, which, ironically, cemented her position as a 'sex kitten', particularly in the USA.

The film made Bardot an international star and although she was immensely popular in America, she continued to make French-language films in Europe. During the 1960s she worked with a number of respected directors, notably, Louis Malle on *Vie Privée* (*A Very Private Affair*, 1961) and Jean-Luc Godard on *Contempt* (1963). She also embarked on a singing career, working principally with Serge Gainsbourg. She recorded the notorious *Je t'aime . . . moi non plus*, but pleaded with him not to release the duet, so he made a new version with Jane Birkin, which became an international hit in 1969. Bardot came to epitomize French glamor and in 1970 was used as the model for the bust of Marianne, the French national emblem.

She appeared in over 50 films before her retirement from the screen in 1973. Since then, Bardot has used her celebrity to campaign for animal rights. She founded the Brigitte Bardot Foundation for the Welfare and Protection of Animals in 1986, selling many items of jewelry and personal possessions to raise funds for it. She has also been surrounded by controversy in the latter part of her career. Famously right wing, she has made public comments about immigration, race-mixing and Islam in France; she has been fined five times for inciting racial hatred. In spite of her political views, she remains a screen legend and is often cited as one of the sexiest film stars in the world.

Right: Bardot in a scene from her notorious 1956 movie, *And God Created Woman*.

Below: In her later years Bardot has devoted her life to animal rights campaigning. In 2005 she launched a campaign to stop the slaughter of seals in Canada.

Overleaf: Bardot at the start of her career as the 1950s sex-kitten.

Founded January 1960
Disbanded 1970

Members:
George Harrison 1943–2001
John Lennon 1940–1980
Paul McCartney 1942–present
Ringo Starr (born Richard Starkey)
1940–present

The Beatles

Perhaps the most famous, commercially successful and critically acclaimed British rock band ever, The Beatles redirected the history of western popular culture and music. Their style was rooted in skiffle and rock, but developed into an innovative, sophisticated and genre-busting musical idiom as the group's songwriting skills, range and musical intelligence grew. Singles hits included *She Loves You*, *Can't Buy Me Love*, and *A Hard Day's Night*, but The Beatles' legacy was assured by a sequence of revolutionary albums.

In their early days as a gifted, wisecracking rock-and-roll group, The Beatles revolutionized the sound and style of British popular music with their original and catchy synthesis of rock music, rhythm and blues. They first appeared in the clubs of Liverpool – their home city – and Hamburg. On the way, they lost two early band members - bassist, Stuart Sutcliffe and drummer, Pete Best. They acquired drummer, Ringo Starr, in 1962 to make up the Fab Four of fame and fable.

Molded by manager Brian Epstein from 1962, they adopted their signature mop-head haircuts and collarless suit-jackets and were signed to the EMI Parlophone label by prescient music producer, George Martin. Their debut album *Please Please Me*, recorded in a single session at the iconic Abbey Road Studios, became their first No. 1 hit. In total, 11 studio albums and 17 singles went on to reach the top spot in the British charts – an astonishing record.

Beatlemania went global, when the band toured the USA in spring 1964 and they entered the movie world with their mock-documentary *A Hard Day's Night* (1964) and its successors *Help!* (1965) and *Magical Mystery Tour* (1967). A succession of landmark albums followed. *Rubber Soul* (1965) featured elements drawn from the contemporary US folk scene and from world music, notably in its use of the sitar, while *Revolver* (1966) further extended their range, from classical to psychedelic rock. The phenomenal concept album *Sgt. Pepper's Lonely Hearts Club Band* (1967) is regularly listed as one of the greatest albums of all time.

A creative period of transcendental meditation at a retreat in India led to *The White Album* (1968, formally called *The Beatles*). However, it also increased personal tensions within the group, which became focused on John Lennon's relationship with the artist, Yoko Ono. Two further acclaimed albums followed, *Abbey Road* (1969) and *Let It Be* (1970), but in April 1970, Paul McCartney announced he was quitting the band and he filed for formal dissolution at the end of the year. All four members went on to make solo albums and McCartney developed a hugely successful post-Beatles career.

In the years that followed the band's dissolution, two tragic events happened. Lennon was killed in 1980 in New York City and George Harrison died of cancer in 2001.

Right: The Fab Four in 1964.

Below: The Beatles wave to thousands of fans at London Airport, 1965. As Paul said, 'We didn't all get into music for a job! We got into music to avoid a job, in truth – and get lots of girls.'

Overleaf: The Beatles (left to right) Ringo Starr, John Lennon, Paul McCartney, and George Harrison show off their MBE medals after their investiture at Buckingham Palace in October 1965.

Boris Becker

A tennis phenomenon, Boris Becker astonished the sports world in 1985, by becoming the first unseeded player and the first German, to win the coveted men's singles title at Wimbledon, aged just 17.

Becker had won his first top-level singles title at the Queen's Club, London, only a fortnight earlier, having turned professional the previous year. When he won at Wimbledon, he was the youngest ever male Grand Slam singles champion. But this was no brief flowering – he went on to cement his reputation by taking the singles title at the Cincinnati Open two months later, in August 1985, again the youngest winner ever. The following year, he successfully defended his Wimbledon title in straight sets against Ivan Lendl and went on to win four more Grand Slams in a sparkling career.

His game was a dramatic, serve-and-volley affair, featuring a powerful and accurate serve, delivered with an unusual rocking movement; its pace earned him the nicknames 'Boom Boom' and 'Der Bomber'. Well built and strong, Becker was also a speedy mover about the court, diving for apparently unreachable volleys and sometimes calling on his powerful forehand to out-hit opponents from the baseline. The fast surfaces of grass and carpet courts suited him best.

After two successive Wimbledon wins, 1987 saw him knocked out in the second round of the tournament, though he was ranked number 2 in the world, while in 1988, he lost in the final to Stefan Edberg. Perhaps his best year was 1989, when he clinched two Grand Slam singles wins over his two main rivals, Edberg at Wimbledon and Lendl at the US Open. This, with his sterling performance for Germany in the Davis Cup, led the ATP World Tour to crown him Player of the Year.

However, the world number 1 slot eluded Becker for almost the whole of his career, apart from a brief period in 1991, after he defeated Lendl to win the Australian Open for the first time. Pete Sampras deprived him of a Wimbledon win in 1995, but he took his sixth Grand Slam title the following year, beating Michael Chang in the final of the Australian Open.

Becker was an emotional as well as a dramatic player, whose readily recognizable strokes have led to a whole new terminology among fans and commentators – from the 'Becker Blocker', his early return shot, through the 'Becker Hecht', his flying lunge, to the 'Becker Shuffle', his dance of triumph after an important point.

Since his retirement from professional tennis, Becker has had a successful career as a businessman and tennis commentator.

Born Boris Franz Becker
November 22, 1967
Leimen, Federal Republic
of Germany

Above: Becker celebrates his third victory in the Mens' Singles at Wimbledon, 1989. His previous wins were in 1985 and 1986.

Left: Becker demonstrates his extraordinary reach, here defeating Ivan Lendl in 1985.

David Beckham

Born May 2, 1975
London, England

One of the great soccer legends of the early 21st century, David Beckham has enjoyed a global career. He has played with some of the best clubs in the world, as well as achieving every English footballer's dream of captaining the national squad. At one time the world's highest paid footballer, he was also the first to play in 100 Champions League matches.

Beckham was born in Leytonstone in east London and signed for Manchester United, the club he idolized, as a trainee in 1991. He was a dedicated player, constantly working to improve on his exceptional natural ability and was quickly rewarded with a place in the first team squad in 1992, making his Premier League debut in 1995. Sir Alex Ferguson, the manager of Manchester United, has always believed in exploring the talent of the club's young players and Beckham was fortunate to be one of a group of players nicknamed 'Fergie's Fledglings.'

He repaid his manager's faith many times over, probably most dramatically at the start of the 1996 season when, playing as a midfielder, he scored a goal from the halfway line against Wimbledon, a remarkable feat, unmatched even by the legendary Pelé Beckham was a vital member of Manchester United's team during the record-breaking 1998–9 season, when they achieved the triple crown of winning the Premiership, the FA Cup and the European Cup. Beckham's best season with United was in 2001–2, when he scored 11 goals in 28 league appearances.

In 2003, he moved to Real Madrid in a £25 million deal and in 2007, announced his move to California to play for the Los Angeles Galaxy team, a move that many believed would signal the end of his soccer career. However, Beckham bounced back and in 2009, was on loan to Italian side Milan.

Beckham made his first appearance for England in 1996 and from 1998 was a regular member of the squad. He was captain of the national side from 2000 to 2006 and by 2009, was the country's most capped player, with 115 appearances for the national team. Vilified and adored in almost equal measure during his 14-year England career, Beckham has rescued England more than once with his trademark curving goals and penalties.

Personable and handsome, Beckham pursues his soccer career side-by-side with his life as a dedicated ambassador for British sport in general and as an international celebrity (thanks in no small part to his wife, former Spice Girl, Victoria). He has also been generous with his support for young players with the establishment of the David Beckham Football Academies in London and Los Angeles. But it is his soccer exploits, his determination, passion and professionalism, that have made him one of the best players in the history of the beautiful game.

Right: Beckham playing for Real Madrid in June 2007.

Below: Away from the football pitch, David and Victoria Beckham are international celebrities and are highly sought-after by fashion designers, health and fitness specialists and others who want them to endorse their products.

The Bee Gees

Established 1958

Members:
Barry Gibb 1946– Present
Robin Gibb 1949– Present
Maurice Gibb 1949–2003

In a long and checkered career, The Bee Gees have survived changing fashions, derision and adulation to earn a place as one of the most influential bands of the late 20th century.

Born in Douglas on the Isle of Man, the Gibb brothers were brought up in Queensland, Australia, where they began to perform as a singing trio. The Bee Gees have enjoyed two main phases of popularity. The first, in the late 1960s, produced (among others) the singles *New York Mining Disaster* and *To Love Somebody* - a plaintive ballad that has since been covered by hundreds of artists, including Nina Simone, Janis Joplin and Michael Bolton. In 1969, Robin Gibb left to go solo, but the brothers reunited in 1971 and early in 1975, recorded *Jive Talkin*, the first record to feature what became their signature falsetto sound. The release of the soundtrack to the 1977 movie *Saturday Night Fever* made the Bee Gees global stars. Their vocals featured the trademark high-pitched Bee Gee harmonies, together with a fast moving disco beat and the brothers Gibb were photographed in clinging white shirts, with a flash of medallion nestling below their beards and their dazzling white teeth, framed by flowing locks. *Stayin' Alive*, *How Deep is Your Love*, *Tragedy* and *You Should be Dancing* defined the disco era and the album *Saturday Night Fever* sold over 40 million copies, becoming the biggest selling soundtrack album at the time of its release.

As the disco era faded into a much-mocked memory, The Bee Gees' popularity declined, but their songwriting skills remained as strong as ever. Nothing they released in the 1980s was as successful as their 1970s output and the brothers suffered from an image problem as much as anything – popular taste had simply changed. Only *You Win Again* (1987) came near to recapturing their earlier commercial success.

During the 1990s, they produced several successful records and launched a series of 'One Night Only' concerts around the world, despite Maurice's battle with alcoholism and Barry's arthritis, which threatened to end his guitar playing. Nostalgia for their distinctive sound meant that by the turn of the century they had recaptured both critical and commercial success.

Sadly, Maurice died suddenly in 2003 in Miami, Florida. The two surviving brothers celebrate some 50 years in show business, with over 120 million albums sold worldwide, their detractors are forced to acknowledge The Bee Gees' astonishing success as prolific songwriters and one of the most popular bands of all time. Their longevity is a tribute to their unerring skills as songwriters – over 2,000 artists have recorded their songs, an extraordinary tribute to their versatility and talent.

Left: The Bee Gees have sold over 205 million records and singles during the course of their 50-year career.

Below: Although Barry Gibb claimed, 'I never really did any disco dancing,' The Bee Gees are forever associated with the disco era of the 1970s.

Beyoncé

Singer, actor and all-round international superstar, Beyoncé Knowles seemed destined for success from an early age. From the start of her professional career with the all-girl group, Destiny's Child, to her solo projects, Beyoncé has projected a highly polished stage presence that dazzles her fans. She has sold an astonishing 100 million records and is the most successful female artist of the 2000s.

As a child, Beyoncé demonstrated an extraordinary musical talent and, despite her shyness, was a natural performer at her jazz and ballet classes. By the time she was in high school, she was singing in a band with her cousin, Kelly Rowland, and friends, LaTavia Roberson and LeToya Luckett. Named Girl Tyme, they grew in professionalism as a rapping and dancing band, and were managed and promoted by Beyoncé's father. In 1997, their name changed to Destiny's Child, the band signed a record deal with Columbia and their first single, *No, No, No* was released in 1998. Their second album *The Writing's on the Wall* (1999) was their breakthrough and provided their first Number One single, *Jumpin' Jumpin'* as well as the song that became their signature, *Say My Name.*

With their energetic, lively performances, Destiny's Child made a tremendous impact on the world of R&B. By 2001 it became clear that Beyoncé was the star of the show and she edged ever closer to solo stardom with the

Born Beyoncé Giselle Knowles
September 4, 1981
Houston, Texas, USA

singles, *Independent Women Part 1*, from the *Charlie's Angels* soundtrack, and the 2001 chart-topping album, *Survivor*.

Finally, in 2002, Beyoncé co-starred as Foxxy Cleopatra in the movie *Austin Powers in Goldmember*, and released her first solo single, *Work it Out* from the soundtrack. She went on to record songs with rapper Jay-Z and won Grammys with Luther Vandross for their duet, *The Closer I Get to You* and *Dance with My Father*.

Two more films in 2006 established her as a talented actor; *The Pink Panther*, and more famously, *Dreamgirls*, for which she received two Golden Globe nominations. Based on the story of Diana Ross and the Supremes, *Dreamgirls* inspired her next album, *B'Day*, which she co-wrote and produced in just three weeks.

Committed, inspired and hard-working, Beyoncé does not let the grass grow under her feet, juggling concerts, albums and promotions in a schedule that would exhaust lesser mortals. She and her mother launched a fashion line, the House of Deréon, in 2005, and she is a generous philanthropist to several charities. She is a deeply private person, hiding her marriage to Jay-Z in 2008 and adopting a detached view of her feisty stage persona, that she privately called Sasha Fierce. Her third album, *I am . . . Sasha Fierce* (2008) allowed her to merge the two aspects of her music, mixing mainstream songs with R&B, to critical and popular acclaim.

Left, right & overleaf: A typically energetic performance from Beyoncé at Philips Arena, Atlanta, Georgia in 2009.

Humphrey Bogart

Born Humphrey DeForest Bogart
December 25, 1899
New York City, USA

Died January 14, 1957
Los Angeles, California, USA

Neither classically handsome, nor especially versatile, Humphrey Bogart was in many ways an unlikely star. Yet 'Bogie' became one of the Hollywood greats, cornering the market in playing tough, world-weary, yet compellingly decent characters. He appeared in 75 films, among them some of the great classics of the 1940s and 1950s, such as *The African Queen*, *The Treasure of the Sierra Madre* and most notably, *Casablanca*.

After military service in the US Navy in World War I, Bogart returned home to New York, where he got a job as a theatrical manager. He made his Broadway acting debut in 1922 and was reasonably successful, playing juvenile leads, or supporting roles. After the Wall Street Crash of 1929, the lights on Broadway dimmed, as the number of stage productions declined. It seemed to the acting community on the East Coast, that fame and fortune were easier to attain in Hollywood. Like many of his contemporaries, Bogart moved to California in search of work.

In 1930 he appeared in his first film, *Up the River*, alongside Spencer Tracy, playing the first of many tough-guy roles. He spent the next five years traveling between Hollywood and Broadway, but finally achieved a breakthrough with *The Petrified Forest* (1936), in which he played Duke Mantee, another ex-con. Critics praised his performance and Warner Brothers signed him as a contract player for $550 a week.

Bogart appeared in a succession of B movies, usually typecast as a cynical, underworld figure. It took him time to graduate to leading roles, but finally, in 1941, John Huston cast him as Roy 'Mad

Dog' Earle in *High Sierra*. Following the success of *The Maltese Falcon*, in which Bogart appeared as the fast-talking detective Sam Spade, he was cast as Rick Blaine, the tortured, world-weary nightclub owner in *Casablanca*. The movie won the Oscar for Best Picture in 1943 and Bogart's performance opposite Ingrid Bergman – his first romantic lead – is one of the most memorable of his career.

Bogart went on to play brave anti-heroes, notably in *To Have and Have Not* (1944), in which he appeared with the young Lauren Bacall. She captivated him and for the first time, Bogart had an affair with his leading lady. They married in 1945.

In the movies of his last years – *The Treasure of the Sierra Madre* (1948), *The Caine Mutiny* (1954) and *The African Queen* (for which he won an Oscar in 1951) – Bogart gave some of his best

performances. His early death from cancer, at the age of 57, ended one of the most interesting careers in Hollywood. Bogart's restrained, yet compelling, screen presence set him apart from other actors and his intelligent and reliable performances gave him a lasting and powerful appeal to generations of movie lovers.

Right: Bogart with co-star Lauren Bacall on the set of *To Have and Have Not*, 1944.

Below: Bogart with Ingrid Bergman in the final scene of the iconic movie, *Casablanca*.

David Bowie

One of the most innovative rock stars of the 1970s and 1980s, David Bowie succeeded in presenting not one, but several iconic faces to the public.

From the androgynous Ziggy Stardust to the glittering Aladdin Sane and on to the ascetic Thin White Duke, Bowie reinvented his image several times during his career. Yet in these different guises, time and again, Bowie proved that he was more than capable of producing arresting songs that wowed his fans and exercised an enormous influence over his peers. Unafraid to experiment with different musical styles, Bowie has enjoyed amazing commercial success, as well as critical acclaim. Throughout his 40-year career he has sold over 136 million albums and remains in the top ten best-selling acts in British pop history. He has recorded with some of the best singers in the business, from Bing Crosby to Mick Jagger and Queen, as well as appearing in over 30 movies.

Born David Jones in south London, Bowie changed his surname early in his career to avoid being mistaken for Davy Jones of The Monkees. The single *Space Oddity*, released to coincide with the moon landing of 1969, was a top five hit in the UK and kick-started Bowie's years of fame. His albums *The Man Who Sold the World* (1970) and *Hunky Dory* (1971) demonstrated a wide variety of musical influences and styles, from the charming, if fey, *Kooks*, through the raw *Song for Bob Dylan* to *Queen Bitch*, one of the earliest glam rock numbers. The concept album *The Rise and Fall of Ziggy Stardust and the Spiders from Mars* (1972) pushed the glam rock theme still further, with Bowie resplendent in sparkling jump suits, flamboyant make-up and a red mullet hairstyle. A year later, he

achieved his first No. 1 album in the UK with *Aladdin Sane* and for the publicity, maintained his persona as Ziggy Stardust. But he soon left Ziggy behind and his work became more soul-based on *Young Americans*. Next came a diversion into the electro-synthesizer world of the Thin White Duke – an extension of the character Bowie played in the 1976 cult science fiction movie *The Man Who Fell to Earth* – on Station to Station and the three albums known as the 'Berlin Trilogy' (1977–9).

During the early 1980s, he moved on yet again, writing commercially popular rock numbers for *Let's Dance* in 1983. He formed a new band, Tin Machine, in 1989, which received a lukewarm reception, in contrast to his immensely popular 'Sound and Vision' stadium tour of 1991. True to form, he experimented with grunge, rap, dance and Indie music

Born David Robert Haywood Jones
January 8, 1947
London, England

in the 1990s and early 2000s with varying degrees of success.

Bowie stands out among pop stars as a writer of intellectual rigor, great imagination and terrific innovation. Few have reinvented themselves so often and so successfully, while pursuing a long career at the top of their field.

Left: Ziggy Stardust, David Bowie's alter-ego during the 1970s.

Below: David Bowie assumed a more sophisticated and suave persona during the *Let's Dance* years of the early 1980s.

Marlon Brando

Born Marlon Brando Jr.
April 3, 1924
Omaha, Nebraska, USA

Died July 1, 2004
Los Angeles, California,
USA

Marlon Brando's brooding good looks and carefully considered 'Method' acting first brought him acclaim in the 1950s and he is still seen as one of the finest Hollywood actors of all time. His performances in *A Streetcar Named Desire* (1951) and *On the Waterfront* (1954) catapulted him to the Hollywood A list and the picture of him astride his Triumph motorbike in *The Wild One* (1953) is one of the most iconic images in cinema history.

Brando was born in Omaha, Nebraska and after dropping out of high school and military academy, moved to New York. There he studied acting at the New School, under the influential Lee Strasberg and Stella Adler. He made his Broadway debut in 1944 and was voted Broadway's Most Promising Actor in 1946 for his role in *Truckline Café*. His breakthrough came with his magnetic and influential performance as Stanley Kowalski in the original 1947 production of Tennessee Williams' play *A Streetcar Named Desire*, which propelled him from Broadway to Hollywood. He played the same role on film in 1951, which won him an Oscar nomination for Best Actor.

His third Hollywood movie, *The Wild One* (1953), projected the unforgettable image of a leather-clad biker Brando on to the public consciousness. The malign influence of the angry, rebellious young man was viewed with trepidation and the film was actually banned for 14 years in Britain.

Brando won his first Oscar for *On the Waterfront* (1954) and then tried to work against type in a series of movies that demonstrated his range and versatility: he took to song-and-dance routines in *Guys and Dolls* (1955), tackled a serious

historical subject as Napoleon in *Désirée* and played an effete Fletcher Christian in *Mutiny on the Bounty* (1962). *Mutiny* reinforced Brando's reputation as a difficult actor and the film shoot went massively over budget and deadline, partly because Brando took over as director.

None of Brando's work in the 1960s was received with much enthusiasm by either critics, or audiences, but his portrayal of the Mafia boss Don Vito Corleone, in the classic 1972 movie *The Godfather* demonstrated a return to his earlier form. It also earned him his second Oscar – which he declined for political reasons. He received a seventh Oscar nomination for his performance in Bernardo Bertolucci's *Last Tango in Paris* (1973), which has been described as the best of his career. It turned out to be his last critically acclaimed movie, though there were cameo roles in *Apocalypse Now* (1979) and *Superman* (1978).

Brando's eccentricities and chronic weight problems meant that he worked only intermittently for the rest of his life. However, acknowledged by his peers as a great actor, his influence still permeates Hollywood. 'The only thing an actor owes his public is not to bore them' he once remarked and he could never be accused of that.

Left: *The Wild One*, 1953.

Below: As Stanley Kowalski in *A Streetcar Named Desire*.

James Brown

Born James Joseph Brown Jr.
May 3, 1933
Barnwell, South Carolina,
USA

Died December 25, 2006
Atlanta, Georgia, USA

Famous for his flamboyant, energetic and passionate performances, James Brown was one of the most successful black artists of the 1960s and 1970s.

His funky soul hits brought dance music alive and made him one of the most original and influential artists in 20th-century music. Only Elvis Presley enjoyed more US chart entries than Brown. He was a prolific writer and much-imitated performer, with some 800 songs in his repertoire. As 'the Godfather of Soul', he also worked tirelessly throughout his career, earning himself another title, 'the hardest working man in show business.'

Born in South Carolina, during the segregation era, James Brown had a difficult and impoverished upbringing. He ended up in jail at the age of 16, after being convicted of an armed robbery.

While in prison, he learned to sing and perform with the prison gospel group and on his release, he joined a group called the Gospel Starlighters. They moved into secular music, renamed themselves the, Famous Flames and scored an R&B Top Ten hit in 1956, with *Please, Please, Please*, penned by Brown. For the next few years, Brown recorded gospel-inspired R&B music, combining frenzied lead vocals with complicated backing riffs. His first mainstream hit came in 1962 with the release of *Night Train* and in 1963 he achieved national recognition with his live album, *Live at the Apollo*, which sold an astonishing one million copies.

Brown became famous for his dramatic and well-choreographed stage acts. He also broke out of the restrictive mold of black R&B by establishing his own production company, Fair Deal, to promote his work more widely. The complex rhythms of his songs and the repetition of vocal phrases proved hugely influential in the world of funk music, but he also achieved mainstream success with two songs in 1965 and 1966 that came to define his act – *Papa's Got a Brand New Bag* and *I Got You (I Feel Good)*.

In the era of the Black Power movement in the USA, Brown added his voice to that of other black celebrities. He recorded *Say it Loud – I'm Black and Proud* in 1968, as well as lending a calming presence to the race riots that erupted in the wake of Martin Luther King's assassination.

By the early 1980s a younger generation of rap and hip hop artists, heavily influenced by Brown, was displacing him. Brown switched his talents to the movies and continued to tour relentlessly. His colorful private life merely added to his legendary status as one of the most exciting performers in the world. His concert performances were renowned – long, loud, visual extravaganzas with vigorous dance routines and unforgettable vocals. He continued performing right up to his sudden death on Christmas Day 2006.

Right: The Godfather of Soul in 1981.

Left: Brown performing at the Rock and Roll Hall of Fame show, 1995.

Richard Burton

Born Richard Jenkins
November 10, 1925
Pontrhydyfen, Wales

Died August 5, 1984
Céligny, Switzerland

With his rich, mellifluous tones and commanding stage presence, Richard Burton was one of the finest British actors of the 1950s and 60s. Nominated seven times for an Academy Award (but never winning), he was a passionate actor, as well known for his on-off relationship with his second wife, Elizabeth Taylor, as for his acting roles.

Burton was the twelfth of 13 children. His mother died giving birth to the last child, and young Richard Jenkins was brought up by his older sister and her husband. He was mentored by one of his schoolteachers, Philip Burton, who regarded Richard as a son and nurtured his passion for language and his talent for acting. When he began his acting career, Richard adopted Philip Burton's surname as a tribute to his teacher.

Once he was discharged from the RAF after National Service in 1947, Burton began acting professionally full-time and appeared in his first film in 1948, *The Last Days of Dolwyn*. He also began a stage career, appearing alongside Sir John Gielgud and Clare Bloom in *The Lady's Not for Burning* in 1949. Good-looking, intelligent and with a measured stage presence, Burton was praised by the critics; this helped win him the role of Prince Hal in Shakespeare's *Henry IV Part I* at Stratford in 1951. Burton found himself in the middle of British acting, and through these connections, made the leap to Hollywood in 1952.

Burton received the first of seven Academy Award nominations for his first film, Daphne du Maurier's *My Cousin Rachel* (1952), in which he appeared opposite Olivia de Havilland. His performance in *The Robe* the following year prompted Hollywood producer Daryl Zanuck to offer him a $1 million, seven-year contract.

In 1954, Burton's distinctive voice earned him his most famous radio role, narrating Dylan Thomas's *Under Milk Wood*. Acclaimed as a one of the most promising Shakespearean actors of his generation, Burton juggled stage and screen work at the end of the 1950s and in 1960 he started filming *Cleopatra*, in which he played Mark Antony opposite Elizabeth Taylor's Cleopatra. Burton and Taylor's relationship overshadowed the troubled production, and their marriage in 1964 catapulted Burton into the league of Hollywood royalty, enabling him to command vast salaries for subsequent films. Burton and Taylor starred together in a number of films, notably *Who's Afraid of Virginia Woolf* (1966) and Zeffirelli's *The Taming of the Shrew* (1967). Burton's 1968 role with Clint Eastwood in *Where Eagles Dare* finally cast him in a commercial blockbuster.

During the 1970s, interest in his lifestyle tended to overshadow his acting and having not won an Oscar it seemed he never fulfilled his early promise. Sadly, Burton died from a brain hemorrhage in 1984, aged only 58.

Left: In 1953 Burton starred as Hamlet at the Old Vic theater in London.

Below: Burton and Taylor at a charity performance of prose and poetry in New York in 1964.

Overleaf: Richard Burton and Elizabeth Taylor on the set of the 1965 movie *The Sandpiper*.

Tim Burton

Born August 25, 1958
Burbank, California, USA

Tim Burton is one of the most successful film directors of recent years, famous for his quirky, imaginative and original movies that appeal to adults and children alike.

Raised in California, Burton claims to have spent much of his childhood as a recluse, drawing cartoons and watching old movies, especially those starring his hero, Vincent Price. He attributes much of the bleakness in his films to his reaction to growing up in suburban Burbank. Fascinated by monster movies, Burton studied animation before working for Disney, where he acquired a solid grounding in the mechanics of animation and film-making.

Burton's personal ambitions and imagination were some what removed from Disney's wholesome output, however, and in 1982 he made his first short movie, entitled *Vincent*. A black and white stop-motion film, it is about a young boy who dreams about his hero, Vincent Price, with Price himself providing the voiceover. *Frankenweenie*, Burton's 1984 parody and homage to the 1931 *Frankenstein* movie, attracted a varied amount of publicity, most immediately from his bosses at Disney who fired him for wasting company resources on a film that they didn't believe was family-friendly.

But Burton's unorthodox, yet appealing and humorous style won him many admirers and he was asked to direct *Pee-Wee's Big Adventure* in 1985 - his first movie that crossed over into the mainstream. He followed this with his first blockbuster, *Beetlejuice* (1988), a dark comedy fantasy that labeled Burton a (bankable) director and a safe pair of hands for box office success.

Batman (1989) seemed like a departure for Burton, as it was a big budget movie of a much-loved subject. Burton played with the dark side of the superhero and delivered a critically acclaimed movie that became one of the biggest earners of all time and won an Academy Award for Best Art Direction. He directed subsequent blockbuster titles, *Batman Returns* in 1992 and *Planet of the Apes* in 2001, but it seems that his heart remains with more off-beat movies.

Batman's success enabled Burton to tackle the type of movies that he loved– gothic fantasies with comedic undercurrents, filmed against beautifully rendered artistic sets. *Edward Scissorhands* (1990) and *The Legend of Sleepy Hollow* (1999) epitomized this style, but Burton recreates these themes time and again with films, such as *Big Fish* (2003) and *Sweeny Todd* (2007). Burton's films frequently focus on people who struggle to fit in with society, as he himself has said, 'I always liked strange characters.' His productions of *Charlie and the Chocolate Factory* (2005) and *Alice's Adventures in Wonderland* (2010) were both directed with his customary verve and imagination. He has also returned to the stop-motion movies of his youth, producing and writing *The Nightmare Before Christmas* in 1993 and directing *The Corpse Bride* (2005).

Burton is an amazingly loyal director and has gathered around him a collection of actors with whom he often collaborates – Johnny Depp, Winona Ryder, composer Danny Elfman and his partner, Helena Bonham Carter. A talented artist who carries a sketchpad almost everywhere, his creative vision shines through into all of his films.

Left: Burton attends the premier of his 2010 movie *Alice in Wonderland* with his partner, English actress Helena Bonham Carter.

Right: Original and inventive, Tim Burton was honored by his peers in 2009 when the Museum of Modern Film Art presented 'A Tribute to Tim Burton' at MOMA in New York City.

Sir Michael Caine

Born Maurice Joseph Micklewhite
March 14, 1933
London, England

Michael Caine is one of the most distinctive, commanding and successful actors of his generation. He has appeared in over 100 movies and been nominated for Academy Awards six times - once in every decade of his long movie career.

Born in London's East End, Caine left school at 15 and served in the army during his National Service, seeing combat during the Korean War. Having dreamed of being an actor while growing up, he spent many years struggling to make a living and, apparently, changed his name from Maurice Joseph Micklewhite to Michael Caine after seeing *The Caine Mutiny*. He worked in repertory theater for a decade, which he has described as 'marvelous training,' before being cast as the stiff-upper-lipped officer in *Zulu* (1963) - the role that propelled him to stardom. He consolidated this success with the role of Harry Palmer, the Cold War spy in *The Ipcress File* (1965) and its sequels. During the 1960s he became a household name and cornered the market in playing rough Cockney diamonds, notably in his Oscar-nominated role as the eponymous *Alfie* in 1966.

Caine is a prolific actor, and has appeared in many films, such as *Jaws: The Revenge* (1987), that critics may say were not worthy of his considerable talents. He has defended his choice of roles, saying, 'First of all, I choose the great roles, and if none of these come, I choose the mediocre ones, and if they don't come, I choose the ones that pay the rent.' But he always delivers a solid performance and has appeared in many noteworthy movies that have become classics, such as *Get Carter* (1971), *Sleuth* (1972), in which he starred opposite Laurence Olivier and Woody Allen's *Hannah and her Sisters* in 1986, for which he won his first Oscar. Ironically, he could not collect his Oscar because he was filming *Jaws: The Revenge*, which earned him a nomination for worst supporting actor in the alternative Razzie awards the following year.

Unlike many actors of his generation, Caine has never gone out of fashion, or faded from the screen – he has worked consistently since the 1960s. Although he is known for his cockney accent, he is a versatile performer, equally capable of playing a deadly German paratroop colonel in *The Eagle Has Landed* (1976), a jaded university lecturer in *Educating Rita* (1983) and the paternalist American orphanage director in *The Cider House Rules* (1999 – for which he won his second Oscar). He also possesses fine comic timing, notably with his appearance as Nigel Powers, Austin's father in *Austin Powers in Goldmember* (2002). More recently Caine has appeared in both *Batman Begins* (2005) and *The Dark Knight* (2008) as Bruce Wayne's loyal butler, Alfred.

Caine was knighted by Queen Elizabeth II in 2000 in recognition for his enormous contribution to acting and to the British film industry.

Left: Caine in one of his most famous roles, as the Cold War secret agent Harry Palmer, in *Funeral in Berlin*, 1966. (a sequel to his previous film, The Ipcress File).

Below: In 2000 Michael Caine won the Oscar for Best Supporting Actor for his role in T*he Cider House Rule*s.

James Cameron

Born August 16, 1954
Kapuskasing, Ontario,
Canada

James Cameron has established himself as Hollywood's premier director of some of the most profitable movies in cinema history, such as *The Terminator* (1984), *Titanic* (1997) and *Avatar* (2009). A Cameron movie is characterized by amazingly innovative special effects, backing up a suspense-filled plot.

Cameron is more than just a Hollywood mogul, however. As a child he watched Stanley Kubrick's *2001: A Space Odyssey* many times and it inspired his interest in filmmaking and model making. He has a keen interest in the mechanics of special-effects and, early in his career, he studied the technology of special-effects techniques. A philosophy major in college, he also studied physics and has always believed in the integration of arts and science in his movies.

Cameron's first professional movie job was as a miniature set builder and art director on the sci-fi film *Battle Beyond the Stars*, in 1980. He worked on the special effects for *Escape from New York* in 1981, before securing the job of special-effects director on *Piranha II: The Spawning* after the movie's director left. The job was a challenging one, with a minimal budget and a crew that spoke little English. He claims that the stress of the job prompted nightmares, which he turned into a screenplay for his next movie, about a robot assassin from the future: *The Terminator*.

Having written the screenplay, Cameron struggled to find a studio that would let a comparatively inexperienced director direct the movie, but Orion Pictures took the risk and were rewarded for doing so. Costing £6.5 million dollars to make, *The Terminator* starring Arnold Schwarzenegger, earned $78 million at the box office.

Cameron had established himself, and went on to write and direct a succession of blockbusters: *Aliens* (1986), *Terminator 2: Judgment Day* (1991) and *True Lies* (1994). He earned a reputation as a perfectionist director who expected equally high standards and commitment from his cast and crew. Special-effects work is demanding of both time and money and Cameron frequently went over budget and beyond deadline on his projects. This was especially true of *Titanic*, which was a superlative movie in every sense. Nominated for 14 Oscars, it won 11 and was the most expensive movie ever made at the time. Until the release of *Avatar* in 2009, it was also the highest-grossing film ever released with worldwide box office sales of $1,835,300,000 (£1,238,010,697).

Cameron has always worked at the cutting-edge of movie technology and science fiction is his first love, so it was no surprise that his 2009 movie, *Avatar*, set new standards in special effects and visual techniques. In this film, as in many others, Cameron combined fast action and spectacular effects with a thought-provoking plot and it is this mixture of adventure and intelligence that has made him one of the most arresting film directors of the age.

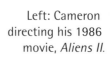

Left: Cameron directing his 1986 movie, *Aliens II*.

Right: Cameron is more than just an amateur sci-fi buff, and is a member of the NASA Advisory Council, helping to advise on public education.

Mariah Carey

Born March 27, 1970
Huntingdon, New York,
USA

Mariah Carey is one of the most successful female recording artists of all time, her unique blend of R&B, pop and soul music, winning millions of fans around the world.

From her debut in 1990, Mariah Carey's powerful five-octave voice and songwriting abilities shot her straight to the top of the music charts. Her first five singles, starting with *Vision of Love*, all reached No. 1 in the Billboard chart – making her the only artist to have achieved this. She has had 18 No. 1 hits in the USA, placing her ahead of Elvis Presley and only just behind The Beatles in the musical league tables.

Carey was born in Huntingdon, Long Island. Her mother was an Irish-American opera singer, her father a black Venezuelan engineer. Her musical talents were clear from childhood, when she copied her mother singing snatches of opera around the house. Moving to New York City at 17, Mariah worked as a waitress, while cutting a demo tape and working as a backing singer. Columbia Records executive, Tommy Mottola, signed her in 1988, immediately after hearing her demo tape and she released her first album, *Mariah Carey*, in 1990. With four No. 1 singles from this album alone, Carey won Grammy awards in 1991 for Best New Artist and Best Female Vocalist. Mottola continued to manage her career and they married in 1993.

Carey became the most successful female singer of the 1990s, selling more than eight million copies of each of her first three albums (*Mariah Carey, Emotions* and *Music Box*) and achieving a series of No. 1 hits. Specializing in emotive ballads and dance pop songs, she is often compared to Whitney Houston, but claims that her greatest influences are Billie Holiday, Gladys Knight and Aretha Franklin. From the mid-1990s she began incorporating elements of hip-hop into her work, telling critics who accused her of trying to exploit a popular genre that she had grown up with the music. She duetted with Boyz II Men on *One Sweet Day* in 1995 and invited rap stars, such as Jay-Z and Snoop Dogg, to guest on a number of singles.

Carey was divorced from Mottola in 1997. After ten years of incessant recording and touring, as well as great commercial success, Carey had a breakdown in 2001; this coincided with unfavorable reviews for her albums *Rainbow* (1999) and *Glitter*, which accompanied a poorly reviewed film of the same name in 2001.

In the early years of the 21st century, it seemed that Carey's crown had slipped, as she was panned for both her singing and her acting. However, she bounced back in 2005 with the release of *The Emancipation of Mimi* and more recently, was much praised for her role in the award-winning movie *Precious* (2009).

Left: Carey performed *Hero* at the Neighborhood Inaugural Ball for President Obama in January 2009.

Below: With five Grammy awards to her name, Carey is one of the most successful female artists of all time.

Johnny Cash

Born February 12, 1932
Kingsland, Arkansas, USA

Died September 12, 2003
Nashville, Tennessee, USA

Johnny Cash's unmistakable deep gravelly baritone made an impact on the world of country music from the start of his career. Although he began recording in the early rock 'n' roll era, Cash remained true to his country roots and resisted the temptation to adopt outside musical influences. He was the first country singer to gain mainstream recognition and, in spite of his strong religious faith, he relished his status as an anti-authoritarian figure. His career spanned nearly five decades and, to many, he personified country music, despite his years out of the limelight in the late 1970s and 1980s. His influence can be felt in country, rock, folk and gospel music, with artists as varied as Neil Young, Mick Jagger and U2 citing him as an inspiration.

Brought up in Tennessee during the Depression, Cash began writing songs and learned to play guitar during his military service in Germany in 1954. He was signed by Sam Phillip's Sun label in Memphis at the same time as Elvis Presley, although Cash threatened to burn out at an earlier age than the 'King of Rock 'n' Roll.' After a number of hits, such as *Cry Cry, Cry* (1955), and his most durable hit, *I Walk the Line* (1956), Cash moved to California in 1958. Although he continued to release successful songs, such as *Ring of Fire* (1963), he became addicted to drink and drugs, nearly suffering a fatal overdose in 1968. He was rescued by June Carter, who helped him and agreed to marry him only once he was clean.

The release of the highly regarded live album *At Folsom Prison* (1968) brought him to international attention and his guest appearance on Bob Dylan's album *Nashville Skyline* (1969) contributed to his rehabilitation. The release of the

humorous *A Boy Named Sue* in the same year (his biggest hit) convinced the world that Johnny Cash had turned himself around. At this stage, Cash was even outselling The Beatles. He rediscovered his Christian faith and embarked on a successful TV series, *The Johnny Cash Show* (1969–71), which introduced a varied mix of artists to television audiences, from the reclusive Bob Dylan, to Louis Armstrong and Kris Kristofferson.

Cash became known as the 'Man in Black' because, in contrast to many of the other rhinestone cowboys of country music, he performed dressed in black, which he said represented his sympathy for 'the poor and the beaten down.' Despite a few brushes with the law, Cash was never imprisoned. During the 1980s he toured with fellow country stars Kris Kristofferson, Willie Nelson and Waylon Jennings as The Highwaymen.

Cash had a commanding stage presence and by the 1990s his work enjoyed a revival sparked by the release of the 1994 album *American Recordings*. Recorded in Cash's living room *American Recordings* featured both new material and covers of songs by artists including Kris Kristofferson, Nick Lowe, Leonard Cohen, Tom Waits and Loudon Wainwright. The album achieved both critical and commercial success,

winning a Grammy for Best Contemporary Folk Album.

Cash died on September 12, 2003 leaving a legacy that ensured his place as one of the outstanding musical influences of the late 20th century. In 2005 Joaquin Phoenix starred as Cash in the biographical film *Walk the Line*.

Below: Cash performing in White Plains, New York, 1959.

Right: 'The Man in Black' playing in 1997, during his career revival of the 1990s.

Coco Chanel

Born Gabrielle Bonheur Chanel
August 19, 1883
Saumur, France

Died January 10, 1971
Paris, France

'Simplicity,' said fashion designer Coco Chanel, 'is the keynote of all true elegance' and this belief underlined all her designs. Her garments were truly timeless – the famous 'little black dress' is still a staple of many wardrobes 80 years after Coco first devised it – and she introduced classic suits and trousers for women, as well as perfect accessories, to the world of fashion.

Chanel deliberately shrouded her early life in mystery and knocked ten years off her age. However, it seems that her mother died when she was 12 and Chanel was sent to an orphanage, where she learned to sew. It may be that the austere black-and-white habits of the nuns influenced the starkness and simplicity of her later designs.

Chanel acquired the nickname 'Coco' during a short career as a cabaret singer from 1905 to 1908. She worked as a seamstress by day and became the mistress of the textile heir, Etienne Balsan. His patronage enabled her to start designing hats and by 1913, she was able to open her first millinery shop. The financial support of a new lover, Arthur 'Boy' Capel, funded new boutiques in Deauville and Biarritz, the coastal playgrounds of wealthy French people in the pre-war years. Next, Chanel introduced women's sportswear, an entirely new concept, which allowed women to wear practical clothing for outdoor activities.

It was Chanel's move into haute couture from 1918 that revolutionized women's fashion in the first half of the 20th century. The role of women in society had changed during World War I, as they acquired a new independence. Chanel's designs both reflected and encouraged this evolution, replacing the corsets and restrictive clothing of the Victorian era with innovative, elegantly designed clothes. Many of her designs were inspired by menswear and were made up in jersey fabric, which was simple, practical and – best of all for the cash-strapped designer – cheap.

By the mid-1920s, Chanel's reputation as an inspired couturier was well established. Her boutique in Paris's rue Gambon sold simple daywear, classic blazers, suits, sailor tops and straight skirts, as well as lace and tulle evening gowns. She also introduced the signature Chanel No. 5 perfume in 1921, explaining that perfume 'is the unseen, unforgettable, ultimate accessory of fashion ... that heralds your arrival and prolongs your departure.'

Chanel's departure from Paris was itself prolonged after World War II, when public anger at her close wartime relations with a member of the Nazi regime forced her into exile in Switzerland. But she returned in 1954, aged 70 and ignoring the criticism of the fashion press, resumed her place as a style icon. 'Chanel – above all else – is a style,' she once said. 'Fashion, you see, goes out of fashion. Style never.'

Right: 'Luxury must be comfortable, otherwise it is not luxury.' Wise words from the perfectly groomed Coco Chanel, who was always the image of simple elegance.

Below: Chanel (right) with a client, actress Ina Clare, 1931.

Charlie Chaplin

Born Born Charles Spencer Chaplin
April 16, 1889
London, England

Died December 25, 1977
Vevey, Switzerland

If there is one image that captures the essence of Hollywood, it is Charlie Chaplin's bowler-hatted Little Tramp, the mischievous everyman figure he created in the days of silent movies.

Chaplin was born into poverty in south London and his life encapsulates the sort of rags-to-riches story so popular with movie fans. The son of an alcoholic father and incapable mother, he rose by sheer talent and hard work to become the most acclaimed actor of his generation and one of the best-known movie stars in the world.

Chaplin performed in music hall and vaudeville in London as a child. After touring the United States with the Fred Karno troupe, from 1910 to 1912, he decided to remain there. He quickly got a job with Mack Sennett's Keystone Film Company, although he found it hard to make the move from stage to screen acting. He persevered, though and the Little Tramp made the first of 35 short-film appearances in 1914, in *Kid Auto Races at Venice*. With his trademark baggy suit, bowler hat, mustache and twirling cane, the Little Tramp became the most popular character of the silent movie era, epitomizing the struggle of the underdog against authority.

Chaplin's early work for Keystone relied on physical slapstick for much of its humor. In 1919, in a bid to break out and exert more creative control, he founded the United Artists company with Mary Pickford, Douglas Fairbanks and the film director, D.W. Griffith. He moved from short movies to acting, producing and directing feature-length films: he released *The Kid* in 1921, but only three more, including his masterpiece, *The Gold Rush*

(1925), between 1923 and 1929. Famously a perfectionist, Chaplin re-shot scenes many times, until they were exactly right. He rarely worked from a script, tending to improvise his films around single ideas and allowing the narrative to build gradually.

Chaplin did not let the advent of sound in 1927 alter his film-making technique. He made three more silent movies, *The Circus* (1928), *City Lights* (1931) and *Modern Times* (1936), before his first talkie, *The Great Dictator* (1940), his defiant send-up of Hitler and the Nazis. At the first Academy Awards ceremony in 1929, he was given a Special Award 'for versatility and genius' in producing *The Circus*.

Chaplin did not hide his left-leaning political views and his colorful private life was a poorly kept secret. But in 1952, during the anti-communist era of McCarthyism in the USA, he was accused of 'un-American activities' and spent the rest of his life in Switzerland. He returned to America only once, to receive an honorary Oscar in 1972. Angered by the reaction of his adopted country, Chaplin satirized American

politics and society in his last leading role, in *O* (1957). Nevertheless, he is forever associated with the early days of Hollywood and remains the most respected actor and director of that era.

Left: Chaplin in his iconic role as the Little Tramp, with actor Jackie Coogan in the classic silent movie, *The Kid*.

Below: Charlie Chaplin in a scene from his 1918 film *Shoulder Arms*.

Cher

Born Cherilyn Sarkisian
May 20, 1946
El Centro, California, USA

Right: Demonstrating an uncanny talent for seeking out the limelight, Cher wears a show-stopping costume at the Academy Awards, 1986.

Below: Cher began her career alongside first husband, Sonny Bono, during the 1960s and early 1970s.

Remarkable for her long career in the entertainment industry, Cher has survived thanks to her natural talent, sheer hard work and a chameleon-like ability to reinvent herself. As a singer, actress, director and record producer, she has won major awards for her work in films, music and television.

Born in California, Cher began her musical career as a session singer at the age of 17 and began working for record producer, Sonny Bono. The pair quickly formed a highly successful personal and professional partnership, marrying in 1964 and releasing their first smash hit, *I Got You Babe*, in 1965. They projected a psychedelic, soft rock image, with Cher as the wise-cracking, exotically dressed half of the duo and Sonny as the good-natured recipient of her wit. They had a series of hits together, all produced by Sonny, as well as individual solo successes, such as Cher's version of Bob Dylan's *All I Really Want to Do* (1965).

As their record sales declined at the end of the 1960s, Sonny tried (unsuccessfully) to launch their film career, but he had more luck with a series of Las Vegas shows, which paved the way for an immensely successful TV career, notably the *Sonny and Cher Comedy Hour* (1971–4). Meanwhile, Cher continued with her recording career, achieving several No. 1 hits, such as *Gypsys, Tramps & Thieves* (1971) and *Dark Lady* (1974).

Sonny and Cher's marriage disintegrated very publicly in 1975 and Cher's solo career entered a lackluster phase. It was acting, Cher's first love, that relaunched her career in the 1980s and earned her a number of plaudits – from a Golden Globe nomination for *Come Back to*

the Five and Dime, Jimmy Dean, Jimmy Dean (1982), to an Oscar for Best Actress in 1988 for her performance as a homely clerk in the romantic comedy, *Moonstruck*. Nominated for Best Supporting Actress for *Silkwood* in 1984, she also starred in the wickedly funny *The Witches of Eastwick,* alongside Jack Nicholson in 1987.

Cher enjoyed another round of musical success from the end of the 1980s, releasing new albums and internationally popular singles. They included *If I Could Turn Back Time* (1989), whose video was banned from MTV, as Cher performed clad in a characteristically flamboyant

costume, deemed too revealing for TV audiences. Her 23rd album, *Believe* (1998), produced the biggest hit of her long career, as the title track reached the No. 1 spot in 23 countries around the world. Her elaborate live concerts are legendary, typically including complicated choreography and lavish costumes.

Her personal life has been as colorful as her stage costumes and has contributed to Cher's status as one of the great musical divas, as well as a Hollywood legend.

Eric Clapton

Born Eric Patrick Clapton
March 30, 1945
Ripley, Surrey, England

Eric Clapton is one of a handful of iconic British musicians who came of age in the 1960s and continued to produce hits for decades after their initial success. The opposite of the one-hit wonder, Clapton is universally admired as one of the most talented guitarists of his generation.

Clapton learned to play guitar as a teenager and developed his love of blues while at art school in Kingston, Surrey. In 1963, he joined the Yardbirds, a rock band with their roots in Clapton's beloved blues music. Just as they had their first hit, *For Your Love*, in 1965, Clapton left, disillusioned with the band's new pop direction. In the meantime, he had forged a reputation as a tremendously skilled instrumentalist, inspiring a well-known piece of 1960s graffiti, 'Clapton is God.' He played with a succession of R&B bands, before forming Cream in 1966, with Jack Bruce and Ginger Baker.

In the two years of the band's existence, Cream assumed the status of a supergroup, winning both critical and commercial success. For Clapton, this was certainly one of the high points of his long career and allowed him to develop his already impressive technical skills, while also lending his singing voice to hits such as *Sunshine of Your Love* (1968) and *Crossroads* (1969). However, Cream soon broke up in a maelstrom of artistic differences, drink and drugs. After a short spell with Blind Faith, Clapton spent a period guesting with other groups, such as the Plastic Ono Band. He was keen to shrug off his own cult status and appeared embarrassed by the extreme adulation of his fans.

Clapton's heroin addiction may have been his way of coping with the stresses of fame, but it came close to killing him and was succeeded by a heavy dependence on alcohol. Yet despite these personal struggles, he produced some unforgettable records, including the poignant *Layla* (1970), his version of Bob Marley's *I Shot the Sheriff* (1974) and *Wonderful Tonight* (1977).

The release of *Money and Cigarettes* in 1983 signaled a new era for a Clapton, free from the problems of drink and drugs. In 1985, he won a BAFTA for his soundtrack for the BBC thriller *Edge of Darkness*. *Journeyman* (1989) was a collaborative album with George Harrison, Phil Collins and Chaka Khan among others, playing a mixture of blues, pop, jazz and soul.

Clapton continued to play with a variety of his fellow musicians throughout the 1990s, from Roger Waters to Sheryl Crow and B.B. King, both in concert and on albums, such as *From the Cradle*. *Tears in Heaven*, the moving single Clapton wrote after the death of his four-year-old son, won three Grammy awards in 1992.

Frequently cited as one of the most influential guitarists of all time, Clapton is one of rock's great survivors.

Above: A regular performer at charity concerts, Clapton performs alongside Jeff Beck and Jimmy Page.

Left: Clapton performs at a reunion of Cream at Madison Square Garden, 2005.

Kurt Cobain

Born Kurt Donald Cobain
February 20, 1967
Aberdeen, Washington,
USA

Died Died April 5, 1994
Seattle, Washington, USA

Musician and songwriter Kurt Cobain's early death, at the age of 27, ensured his immortality as one of the most significant rock stars of the 1990s.

Heavily influenced by punk and the alternative music of underground and indie groups, Cobain's band, Nirvana, became America's premier grunge group, combining a stadium rock feel with abrasive lyrics. Their hit *Smells like Teen Spirit* (1991) became the anthem of a generation, who came to view Cobain as their spokesman.

Kurt Cobain was born and grew up in a small town, 140 miles south of Seattle. His parents divorced when he was seven, leaving him with feelings of insecurity and anguish that were later to show in Nirvana's music. Given a guitar when he was 14, he taught himself to play and gradually began writing his own songs.

After a false start with his first band, the attractively named Fecal Matter, Cobain formed Nirvana with bass player Krist Novoselic in 1987. They immediately began touring the Seattle area, making little impact. However, their first album, *Bleach*, released in 1989, received a lot of airplay on college radio stations and established the band on the indie scene.

Cobain reveled in the alternative, underground rock roots of Nirvana. He struggled to reconcile his natural dislike of corporate big business with his desire for popular and commercial success. But swallowing their principles in order to get the punk message to a wider audience, Nirvana signed with DGC Records to release their breakthrough album *Nevermind* in 1991. *Nevermind* certainly fulfilled the band's ambitions,

eventually selling 10 million copies in the USA alone and knocking Michael Jackson's *Dangerous* from the No. 1 spot.

The album's first single, *Smells like Teen Spirit*, was swiftly followed by *Come as You Are* and in the first months of 1992, Nirvana became a global phenomenon. Their mainstream success came with all the usual fuss from the media, particularly when Cobain married fellow musician Courtney Love in Hawaii, a few months before their daughter was born. But by the end of that year, despite the personal happiness he had found with his new family, drugs had taken over in Cobain's life. He struggled with a heroin habit from 1991 until the end of his life, overdosing several times.

In 1993, Nirvana's third album, *In Utero*, which *Rolling Stone* magazine described as 'brilliant, corrosive, enraged and thoughtful', shot into the charts at No. 1. The band embarked on a US tour and then went to Europe in early 1994 – a tour that was cut short on March 4 by Cobain's

overdose. He admitted himself to rehab, but committed suicide on April 5, 1994. Kurt Cobain's death provoked shock, anger and grief from his fans and true regret from critics, who admired his angry, thought-provoking music and lyrics.

Right: 'It's better to burn out than fade away', said Kurt Cobain in 1993.

Below: Cobain crowd surfs in his home town of Seattle, Washington, 1990.

Sean Connery

Born Thomas Sean Connery
August 25, 1930
Edinburgh, Scotland

One of Scotland's biggest film stars, Connery most famously made the role of James Bond his own in seven hugely successful and trendsetting films, between 1962 and 1983. His later career, as a much-loved Hollywood professional, has seen him making box office hits well into his seventies.

Legend has it, that Connery was working as a milk delivery man when he landed the role of Bond. In fact, he had played his first stage and film roles in the 1950s and co-starred with Claire Bloom in a TV version of *Anna Karenina* in 1961.

But it was his gritty, sensual, predatory Bond that established not only his own career, but an enduring film character. Author Ian Fleming's creation was a cold-blooded, daring, but rather two-dimensional womanizer; Connery added substance and a sense of humor. The early films, such as *Dr. No* (1962) and *Thunderball* (1965), were genuinely suspenseful and for the time, risqué. Fleming, initially unsure whether Connery was the right man for the role, gave Bond a half-Scottish, half-Swiss background in his later novels, in tribute to the actor.

Connery's later outings in the role, such as *Diamonds Are Forever* (1971), became slightly self-parodying and the films themselves were increasingly spectacular, gadget-oriented and improbably plotted. He had other successful roles while making the Bond films, notably in Alfred Hitchcock's *Marnie* (1964), John Huston's *The Man Who Would Be King* (1975) and Terry Gilliam's *Time Bandits* (1981).

A thoughtful and serious actor, who prepared carefully for his roles, Connery never allowed himself to be typecast and had a series of big hits in the 1980s. These include the popular fantasy *Highlander*, the historical thriller *The Name of the Rose* (both 1986), de Palma's *The Untouchables* (1987), which won him his only Oscar for his crafty Irish cop and *Indiana Jones and the Last Crusade* (1989), in which he played Harrison Ford's father. More recent successes have included roles as an ageing cat burglar in *Entrapment* (1999), a reclusive author in *Finding Forrester* (2000) and a Victorian version of Bond in *The League of Extraordinary Gentlemen* (2003). The last was an unhappy experience, which appears to have hastened his retirement.

In 1989, Connery was voted the Sexiest Man Alive by the US weekly *People* magazine, but official recognition of his services both to film and to British exports was slow to come. His active support for the Scottish National Party, which campaigns for Scottish independence from the UK, is thought to have delayed for many years his long-awaited knighthood, but it finally came in 2000. A major philanthropist, Connery donated his entire salary from *Diamonds Are Forever* – well over $1million – to the Scottish Educational Trust, which he co-founded.

Left: Connery in his most famous role, as James Bond in the first Bond movie, *Dr No*.

Below: In 1989 Connery appeared as Professor Henry Jones, father of Indiana Jones, in *Indiana Jones and the Last Crusade*.

Bill Cosby

Born   William Henry Cosby Jr.
July 12, 1937
Philadelphia,
Pennsylvania, USA

One of the most highly paid and well regarded entertainers in American TV, Bill Cosby has become an icon of American culture, mostly as a result of the award-winning series, *The Cosby Show*, which aired for eight years, from 1984 to 1992.

Born in Philadelphia, Cosby left school at 16 and served in the Navy, before finishing his education at Temple University in Philadelphia. While working in a bar, he discovered his talent for making people laugh and decided to pursue a career in comedy, first appearing on TV in 1963 on *The Tonight Show*. His particular talent was to use stories of his youth and background to amuse his audiences, realizing that universal human situations are a powerful bond between people of different races.

As co-star of the *I Spy* adventure series from 1965, he became a role model for black actors and played a part utterly devoid of racial stereotyping, although critics complained that the series did not address the civil rights issues then gripping America. Cosby was the first African-American to play the lead in a weekly drama, but he was relieved when the series ended and he could retreat to stand-up comedy, where he was free from political interference.

In the early 1970s Cosby maintained a steady TV presence, hosting the animated children's program, *Fat Albert and the Cosby Kids* from 1972 to 1984. It was in this year that his most successful show launched. *The Cosby Show* was a weekly production that went on to become the most popular sitcom of all time on American television. Cosby had a large degree of creative control and drew on his successful comedy routines for the show's ever-popular humor. Ironically, it finally bowed out in 1992 after ratings pressure from another show based on family life, *The Simpsons*.

Cosby has yet to repeat the same success, but he has been far from idle. He appeared in several films in the 1990s, including Robin Williams' *Jack* in 1996 and the TV sitcom *Cosby* ran for four seasons from 1996, featuring Bill as a grumpy old man forced unwillingly into retirement. The author of a number of best-selling books, such as *Fatherhood* (1986), Cosby has also continued to work on the educational projects which have been close to his heart since he attained his doctorate in education in 1976, having used his own show, *Fat Albert*, as his dissertation subject.

Left: A formidable live performer, Cosby began his career in show business as a stand-up comic. He is seen here performing live in 1999.

Below: Cosby on the set of *The Cosby Show* in 1985, talking over a scene with his co-star Tempestt Bledsoe.

Marie Curie

Born Marya Skłodowska
November 7, 1867
Warsaw, Poland

Died July 4, 1934
Passy, France

The Polish-born chemist, Marie Curie, is one of the best-known scientists of her day. Together with her husband, Pierre, she carried out pioneering work in the field of radioactivity (a term she coined) and she was the first person ever to win the Nobel Prize twice.

Marya was the child of teachers in Warsaw, whose families had suffered financial hardship through their support for Polish independence. She began her scientific studies in Warsaw, having first worked as a governess to support herself and then transferred to the University of the Sorbonne, in Paris, in 1891. There she gained degrees in both physics and mathematics, changed her name to Marie and met the Frenchman, Pierre Curie, who was a professor in the School of Physics. They married in 1895 and set up a shared laboratory.

The Curies jointly investigated the nature of radioactivity, building on the research of Marie's older colleague, Henri Becquerel, into the radioactive element, uranium. But it was Marie alone, using the electrometer (which measured electrical charge) invented by her husband, who discovered that uranium emitted radiation by itself and not as a result of interaction with other molecules. She went on to observe that one particular uranium ore emitted much larger amounts of radiation, suggesting to her the existence

of a new element. In July 1898, she and Pierre announced that they had discovered polonium and followed this up in December with the announcement of another element, radium

The Curies received the Nobel Prize for Physics in 1903, for their work on radioactivity, jointly with Becquerel. Marie then worked to isolate radium in appreciable quantities. She continued to work alone after her husband was killed in 1906 in a street accident. In 1911, she was awarded the Nobel Prize for Chemistry for their joint discovery of radium and polonium and for her work on the nature and applications of radium.

World War I provided a grim opportunity to demonstrate the value of the Curies' work. Their research lay behind the vital development of x-rays and Marie campaigned for mobile radiography units, using radium tubes derived from her work to treat the wounded. These became known as 'petites curies.'

As well as her huge contribution to science, Curie was a pioneer in the way she overcame a succession of hurdles placed in her way, because she was a woman. She was the first female teacher at the Sorbonne and after her second Nobel Prize win, she persuaded the French government to fund a Radium Institute, now the Institut Curie. This produced four more Nobel Prize winners, including her daughter Irène Joliot-Curie and son-in-law Frédéric Joliot, who were the first people to produce radioactivity artificially. Marie died of leukemia, caused by her exposure to radiation, the dangers of which were then unknown.

Left: Marie Curie in her laboratory, 1905, two years after winning the Nobel Prize for Physics.

Above: Marie and Pierre Curie formed a remarkable partnership, devoting their lives to their research.

Salvador Dalí

Born Salvador Domingo Felipe
Jacinto Dalí i Domènech
November 29, 1904
Figueres, Catalonia, Spain

Died January 23, 1989
Figueres, Catalonia, Spain

The Spanish surrealist painter, Salvador Dalí, with his trademark moustache, was one of the most famous – and notorious – artists of the 20th century.

Dalí was an eccentric from his earliest days. He spent long childhood hours in a full washtub in the family laundry room, lost in his own imagination. As an adult, he courted attention with a carefully cultivated public persona, once arriving for a function at the Sorbonne in Paris in a Rolls-Royce filled with cauliflowers.

This flamboyant exhibitionism was, he claimed, the source of his creative energies. A naturally skilled draftsman, he painted constantly from his early teens onwards, initially in an Impressionist style, but soon introducing the exuberant color of Fauvist painters, such as Matisse. In 1921, he enrolled at the Madrid School of Fine Arts, where his friends included the film-maker Luis Buñuel and writer Federico García Lorca. Here he learned the meticulous, academic technique that, with his use of color, was to become one of the characteristics of his work. His first one-man show, in 1925, was admired by his fellow-artists, Picasso and Miró.

But it was Dalí's encounter with Surrealism, until then mainly a literary movement, that gave his work its hallucinatory quality and the style for which he is best known: he used everyday images as a means of accessing the subconscious. The result was a major group of paintings in 1929, including two of his most significant works, *The Enigma of Desire* and *The Great Masturbator*. He also developed his theory of the double, or triple image, in which unrelated objects merge and become parts of a whole. So, in *The Phantom Cart* (1933), the driver seems to metamorphose into a tower and in *Mae West* (1934), the star's face is also an almost unfurnished room.

When Dalí's work was introduced to the US, it caused a sensation. His New York exhibition in 1934 included one of his most famous works, *The Persistence of Memory*, with its surreal image of soft, melting watches. In 1940, Civil war in Spain led Dalí to move to the US and a new period of creative activity followed, in which he applied the discoveries of physics to his existing imagery, in works such as *Atomic Leda* (1949) and *Raphaelesque Head Exploding* (1951). He also threw himself into the celebrity lifestyle, designing jewelry and stage sets, painting society portraits and working with movie director Alfred Hitchcock.

In later years, Dalí reverted to Catholicism and began to work with religious subject-matter. He spent the last 40 years of his life back in the Spanish region of Catalonia, where he continued to experiment with novel media – he was one of the first to exploit the artistic potential of holography. He died at the age of 84 in Figueres, the town of his birth, where the fittingly flamboyant Dalí Museum was built to house many of his works.

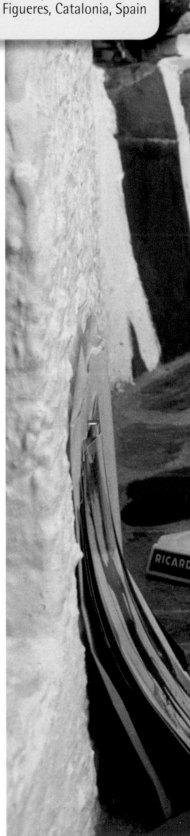

Right: Dali with French singer Amanda Lear at his home in Port Lligat, Spain, 1974. Flamboyant, publicity seeking and extremely astute, Dali cultivated an eccentric image, once saying, 'There is only one difference between a madman and me. I am not mad'.

Bette Davis

Bette Davis, famous for her large, expressive eyes, was one of the most highly regarded actors in Hollywood, capable of playing a wide range of roles and renowned for her forthright style. She appeared in over 100 films and received ten Academy Award nominations, winning Oscars for Best Actress twice.

Davis was encouraged to act by her mother and joined the John Murray Anderson School of Theater, where she studied dance with the legendary Martha Graham. Despite early rejection by director George Cukor, she made her Broadway debut in 1929, where she was spotted by a talent scout and invited to Hollywood for a screen test. Her eyes, which were admired by the cinematographer Karl Freund, won her first part in *The Bad Sister* (1931), but she did not achieve true recognition until her sixth film, *The Man Who Played God* (1932), which earned her a long-term contract with Warner Brothers.

What set Davis apart from many actors was that she was unafraid to tackle difficult roles – she was a true character actor, totally confident in her own abilities. She was not afraid of appearing unattractive, saying of her death scene in *Of Human Bondage* (1934), 'the last stages of consumption, poverty and neglect are not pretty and I intended to be convincing-looking.' Her riveting performance earned critical praise and she won her first Oscar for her next movie, *Dangerous* (1935). In 1936 Davis attempted to break free from being tied to one studio, but was sued by Warner Brothers. The battle paid off, and she was later offered her better roles, playing mature, independent women in films, such as *Jezebel* (1938), *The Little Foxes* (1941) and *Mr Skeffington* (1944).

After several years of mediocre movies, Davis won an Academy Award nomination in 1950 for what has been called the best performance of her career, as the tempestuous Margot Channing in *All About Eve*. However, during the 1950s, both critical and box-office success were elusive and she did not have another major hit movie until 1962, when she starred with Joan Crawford in the classic movie, *Whatever Happened to Baby Jane?* Crawford and Davis were both struggling to revive their careers, and whilst there was no love lost between them, the director Robert Aldrich remarked of the actresses, 'It's proper to say that they really detested each other, but they behaved absolutely perfectly.'

Davis' distinctive, mannered style of acting was much imitated (and occasionally mocked), and audiences appreciated her most when she played the antagonist. She was one of the first actresses to take on roles older than herself, so the transition from starlet to character actress was almost seamless for her. Davis continued to work until the end of her life both in film and television, always admired for her dedication and uncompromising professionalism.

Right: A scene from one of Davis' most famous movies, *Whatever Happened to Baby Jane* (1962). Davis (right) co-starred with Joan Crawford (left).

Born Ruth Elizabeth Davis
April 5, 1908
Lowell, Massachusetts,
USA

Died October 6, 1989
Neuilly-sur-Seine, France

Robert De Niro

Born Robert Mario de Niro Jr.
August 17, 1943
New York City, USA

One of the greatest actors of his time, De Niro made his name in films of often brutal violence, or playing borderline psychotic characters.

The child of artist parents, the part-Italian De Niro discovered his passion for acting when playing the Cowardly Lion in a school production of *The Wizard of Oz*. He studied acting in New York under Lee Strasberg, chief proponent of Method acting, in which actors create convincing performances by generating the thoughts and emotions of their character within themselves. De Niro's first role was in Brian De Palma's comedy *The Wedding Party*, which was made in 1963, but only released in 1969.

It was De Palma who introduced De Niro to movie director, Martin Scorsese. *Mean Streets* (1973) launched De Niro in his guise as a ferocious, unpredictable force of nature, as the wired and terrifying Johnny Boy, alongside Harvey Keitel's Charlie. The two actors have remained good friends ever since.

This was the start of an extraordinarily fruitful partnership with Martin Scorsese and lead roles in a series of electrifying movies, including *Taxi Driver* (1976), *Raging Bull* (1980) and *Goodfellas* (1990). In *Taxi Driver* – perhaps his most famous collaboration with Scorsese – De Niro played the simmering antihero, Travis Bickle, which established him as a star. To prepare for the part, he worked as a cab driver for some months. The musical *New York, New York* (1977) was a departure for both actor and director, with De Niro as the classic leading man, all good looks and charm. But *Raging Bull* returned him to type, in a role for which he put on 30 kilos

(70 pounds) for the later scenes and trained as a boxer for a year. He won two of the three fights he entered, plus a Best Actor Oscar for the role.

Other classic parts included the young Don Vito Corleone in Francis Ford Coppola's *The Godfather, Part II* (1974), for which De Niro mastered a Sicilian dialect and won his first Oscar, for Best Supporting Actor. But he has also ranged way beyond his mafia roles, starring as the deluded and chilling comedian Pupkin in Scorsese's under-rated *The King of Comedy* (1983) and in comedies such as *Brazil* (1985), *Analyze This* (1999), where he spoofs his mafia persona and *Meet the Parents* (2000) and *Meet the Fockers* (2004) with Ben Stiller.

Over the last 20 years, De Niro has also moved into production and heads his

own company, Tribeca. He made his debut as a director with *A Bronx Tale* in 1993 and had a huge success in 2006 with *The Good Shepherd*, starring Matt Damon and Angelina Jolie, about the origins of the CIA.

Right: De Niro on the set of *The Deer Hunter*, 1978. A seering study of the Vietnam war, the movie won the Academy Award for Best Picture, while De Niro was nominated for Best Actor and still claims that it was the most exhausting film of his career.

Below: Filming the 2004 horror movie *Godsend*.

Overleaf: De Niro in one of his most famous films, *Raging Bull*.

James Dean

Angry, vulnerable and disenchanted, James Dean seemed to epitomize the anguish of youth, both for his own and succeeding generations.

Dean's film career lasted less than five years, from January 1951, when he dropped out of university to be an actor, to September 1955 when he was killed in a car crash. And yet in that brief period and in just three roles, he earned his place in the Hollywood constellation of stars, above all with his most celebrated film, *Rebel Without a Cause* (1955). His early death raised him to icon status, as the rebel who died too young.

Raised on a farm in Indiana, Dean moved to California in 1949 and studied drama, before quitting for a series of movie bit-parts. Determined to make his mark, he joined the legendary Actors' Studio in New York, studying Method acting with Lee Strasberg.

A variety of television and stage roles followed and then in 1953, he was picked by director Elia Kazan to play the edgy adolescent Cal Trask in Kazan's movie version (released in 1955) of John Steinbeck's novel *East of Eden*. It is an emotionally complex role: Cal rebels against his puritan father in a classic inter-generational conflict and then discovers that his supposedly dead mother is actually running a nearby brothel.

Dean received a posthumous Best Actor nomination for his role at the 1956 Academy Awards.

But it is for Dean's more central – though just as conflicted – role in Nicholas Ray's *Rebel Without a Cause* that his memory remains eternally fresh. Ray's movie highlights parental failure and troubled youth. At the start, its young hero, Jim, is being held in a police station for public drunkenness. Antagonized by his middle-class parents' mutual hostility and lack of moral strength, he shouts, 'You're tearing me apart' at them. Today it seems a classic teenage tribulation – Jim meets a girl (played by Natalie Wood), becomes mentor to a boy even more confused than himself, falls foul of a gang of bullies and fails to save his friend from dying in a car crash. But in the mid-1950s, it was stunningly new, billing its hero as 'The bad boy from a good family!' The film opened just a month after Dean's own fatal crash: with tragic irony, he was on his way, in his Porsche, to take part in a sports car race – racing being his other passion.

His third film was the sprawling family saga *Giant* (1956), in which, determined not to get typecast, he played an oil-rich Texan, in a support role to Rock Hudson and Elizabeth Taylor. This, too, was nominated for a posthumous Academy Award. But *Rebel Without a Cause* is James Dean's true memorial.

Born	James Byron Dean February 8, 1931 Marion, Indiana, USA
Died	September 30, 1955 Cholame, California, USA

Below: 'Dream as if you'll live forever. Live as if you'll die tomorrow' – poignant words from the young actor, whose career began barely five years before his death in a car crash, aged just 24. Dean is pictured here as Jett Rink, the Texan oil heir, in his last film, *Giant*.

Johnny Depp

Born John Christopher Depp II
June 9, 1963
Owensboro, Kentucky,
USA

Swashbuckling, unconventional and sometimes shocking, Johnny Depp's film roles have been anything but predictable. He has largely avoided blockbusters and brings a benign, humorous, almost mystical aura to all his parts.

Depp's first passion was the guitar. He dropped out of school in 1979 to become a rock musician (he made a solo album in 1997), only later deciding on acting as a career. He made his debut in Wes Craven's creepy, but well-made *A Nightmare on Elm Street* (1984), perhaps a significant precedent for some of the roles that ensued. A number of minor roles followed, but it was the charmingly bizarre *Edward Scissorhands* (1990), his first film with director Tim Burton, which gave him his first real chance to shine. He brought a sense of outcast pathos to a role, that in other hands, might have descended into kitsch.

The relationship with Burton has proved a formative one for them both. They have made seven films together, of which the next was *Ed Wood* (1994), the wacky and unusual story of a film director notorious for writing and directing some of the worst films ever made. *Sleepy Hollow* (1999) was a gothic ghost story in which Depp played detective Ichabod Crane as a delicate, feminine character, at odds with the wild events the film portrays.

Willie Wonka, in *Charlie and the Chocolate Factory* (2005), based on the book by Roald Dahl, was another Burton character created by Depp, while his much praised performance as the titular character in *Sweeney Todd: The Demon Barber of Fleet Street* (2007), based on the Stephen Sondheim musical, gave him his first chance to sing and won him an Oscar nomination for Best Actor. A more recent outing in a Tim Burton movie was the Mad Hatter in *Alice in Wonderland* (2010), which set a new box office record for its opening day's takings.

Beyond his work with Burton, Depp has continued to make interesting and offbeat choices. In a two-year period from 1997 to 1999, he starred in Mike Newell's gangster movie *Donnie Brasco*, Terry Gilliam's *Fear and Loathing in Las Vegas*, the sci-fi shocker *The Astronaut's Wife* and Roman Polanski's tale of decadence among the very rich, *The Ninth Gate*. But perhaps his most iconic role and the one that has cemented his star status, is as Captain Jack Sparrow in the *Pirates of the Caribbean* movies. The first of these was slow to take off at the box office, but the second, *Pirates of the Caribbean: Dead Man's Chest* (2006), grossed a record-making $136 million in its first three days.

Depp himself says that he has a lot in common with Sparrow. In 2007, in gratitude to a London hospital for the care his daughter received there when her kidneys failed, he spent a half day in the children's ward in his Jack Sparrow costume.

Left: Mercurial, unpredictable and always interesting, Johnny Depp has made his name by portraying off-beat, charismatic characters.

Below: As Captain Jack Sparrow from the immensely successful *Pirates of the Caribbean* movies.

Overleaf: Depp arrives at the Venice Film Festival, 2007.

Diana, Princess of Wales

Diana Spencer became, for a time, the most famous woman in the world after her fairytale wedding, in 1981, to the Prince of Wales, heir to the British throne.

The subject of numerous biographies and gossip features, both during and after her scandal-strewn marriage and after her controversial death, Diana remains the pre-eminent female celebrity of her generation. People's princess, English rose, charity campaigner, fashion icon, tragic victim: Diana was all these and an unwitting force for change in the world of the British monarchy.

Diana was born into an aristocratic English family, the granddaughter of the 7th Earl Spencer and became Lady Diana Spencer when her father inherited the title in 1975. Her engagement and marriage were greeted with delight and the wedding in St Paul's Cathedral was watched by an estimated 750 million television viewers worldwide.

Diana was a devoted and hands-on mother to her sons, Princes William and Harry, born in 1982 and 1984 – she fitted her public duties round her children's schedules, in a manner novel to the British royal family. However, she felt stifled and unsupported within the royal entourage. Even before her wedding, she was showing signs of stress and her battle with bulimia continued through much of her marriage.

In the 1990s, that marriage became the subject of feverish public speculation. Both parties used the media to put their case, in a way that permanently altered the relations between British royalty and the press. Stories of Diana's 'hysterical' accusations and suicide attempts were balanced by her increasingly confident and glamorous public persona. Initially demure and traditional, her style developed into that of an international celebrity. Her appearance was carefully considered. She was always able to look right for the occasion, whether wearing waterproofs on deck, Chanel on a state visit to Paris, or a stunning ink-blue creation to dance with John Travolta at the White House.

As her private life crumbled, Diana threw her energies into her increasingly significant charitable work, notably against the use of landmines and for victims of AIDS, at a time when there

Born Diana Frances Spencer
July 1, 1961
Sandringham, Norfolk, England

Died August 31, 1997
Paris, France

was huge social stigma attached to the disease. After her separation (1992) and divorce (1996) from Prince Charles, she ceased to be Her Royal Highness, the Princess of Wales and instead used the title Diana, Princess of Wales. But to the world's media, she remained Princess Di, newsworthy as ever, as they chronicled her increasingly close relationship with Dodi Al-Fayed, playboy son of the owner of Harrods department store in London. Their death together in a car crash in Paris, still the subject of wild conspiracy theories, was probably caused by their driver's attempts to avoid the paparazzi. The extraordinary outpouring of public grief that followed was ample testament to Diana's power to touch hearts worldwide.

Right: 'The People's Princess,' as Diana was dubbed, pictured in October, 1995.

Below: Diana's wedding day, 1981.

Marlene Dietrich

Born	Maria Magdalena Dietrich December 27, 1901 Berlin-Schöneberg, Germany
Died	May 6, 1992 Paris, France

German-born film star of the 1930s, Marlene Dietrich was, according to actor John Wayne, 'The most intriguing woman I've ever known'. Her alluring beauty and assertive personality made her one of the most recognizable stars of the 20th century.

Born in Berlin in 1901, Dietrich studied acting at Max Reinhardt's prestigious drama academy, before acting in small theatrical roles. She appeared in her first film in 1923, *The Little Napoleon,* and went on to make over a dozen German films, as well as appearing on stage in Berlin and Vienna. In 1929, American director Josef von Sternberg cast her as the female lead in *The Blue Angel* and 'discovered' her for the American market. As sultry cabaret singer Lola-Lola she performed what became her signature song, *Falling in Love Again* in her deep, accented voice, which charmed audiences.

Dietrich won a contract with Paramount, who saw her as a rival to MGM's Swedish star Greta Garbo, and she embarked on the most fruitful phase of her career. Her first movie, *Morocco (1930)*, won her an Oscar nomination – all the more remarkable because she spoke very little English and had to learn her lines phonetically. Von Sternberg directed her in six films, which are regarded as some of the most beautifully crafted movies of the 1930s, but they became gradually less commercial with each movie. Sternberg used his exceptional skill in lighting and photography to project Dietrich as the ultimate femme fatale, while coaching her as an actress and ensuring that his sets were technically perfect.

After the box office failure of *The Devil is a Woman* (1935), Dietrich's work dried up for a period, but her career revived in 1939 when she played opposite James Stewart in the Western *Destry Rides Again*. She went on to work with some of the greatest names in Hollywood – Billy Wilder, Fritz Lang, Alfred Hitchcock and Orson Welles – but during the 1940s she devoted much of her time to war work: staunchly anti-Nazi, she became an American citizen in 1939 and from 1941 worked for the war effort, selling war bonds and entertaining troops. In fact, her recording of *Lili Marlene (1945)* was popular with troops on both sides of the conflict.

She appeared in a number of successful postwar films, such as *Witness for the Prosecution* (1957) and *Judgment at Nuremberg* (1961), but from the 1960s, Dietrich worked almost entirely in cabaret. Her finely sculpted cheekbones and deep, husky, slightly accented singing voice giving her a unique appeal that lasted well into old age. She finally gave up performing in 1979 and became increasingly reclusive, refusing to be filmed for the 1984 documentary *Marlene* that she had commissioned from Maximilian Schell. Fiercely private, she remained glamorous and mysterious until the end, retaining her image as a Hollywood icon.

Left: During the 1960s Dietrich enjoyed a successful career as a cabaret performer, maintaining her glamorous appearance as a Hollywood goddess.
Below: During World War II Dietrich worked hard to entertain Allied troops.

Kirk Douglas

Born Issur Danielovitch
December 9, 1916
Amsterdam, New York,
USA

Kirk Douglas was one of Hollywood's leading actors in the years immediately after World War II. Strongly built, with aquiline good looks, he played driven, often cynical characters, always producing an intense, energetic performance.

Douglas' family were impoverished Russian Jewish immigrants to the USA and young Izzy Demsky (as he was known) had to work to pay for his education. He attended the American Academy of Dramatic Arts in New York, where one of his classmates, Betty Perske, later became better known as Lauren Bacall. After serving in the navy during the war, Douglas worked in radio theater, before Bacall recommended him for his first movie, *The Strange Love of Martha Ivers*, in 1946.

Douglas moved to Hollywood and three years later achieved stardom (and his first Oscar nomination) as the ruthless egotistical boxer in *Champion* (1949). He was aware that he did not really suit 'sensitive' parts, and made sure that he chose strong character roles, later saying, 'I don't think I'd be much of an actor without vanity. And I'm not interested in being a modest actor.' He played a variety of roles in the 1950s: a cowboy in *Along the Great Divide* (1951), the manipulative producer in *The Bad and the Beautiful* (1952) and Vincent Van Gogh in *Lust for Life* (1956). He proved that he had fine comic timing when he appeared in Disney's *20,000 Leagues Under the Sea* (1954), playing opposite James Mason's brooding Captain Nemo. Nominated for three Oscars, Douglas was especially annoyed that he was overlooked for *Lust for Life*, which many regard as one of his finest screen performances.

In 1955 he formed his own production company, Bryna Productions and produced two of his most successful movies. In the first, Douglas starred as the French officer Colonel Dax in *Paths of Glory* (1957), directed by Stanley Kubrick and in the second, more famously, was the eponymous rebellious slave in the epic *Spartacus* (1960). Douglas helped to break the Hollywood boycott of alleged communist sympathizers, by using writer Dalton Trumbo on *Spartacus* and ensuring that he was properly credited for his work on the movie.

During the 1960s Douglas appeared in a number of action movies and westerns, such as *The Heroes of Telemark* (1965) and *The Way West* (1967). He brought a special intensity and professionalism to every role he played, believing in the importance of acting as an art form.

He heads an acting dynasty as the father of actor Michael Douglas and producers Peter and Joel Douglas. He was honored with an honorary Academy Award for Lifetime Achievement in 1996, which cited his '50 years as a moral and creative force in the motion picture community.'

Right: Kirk Douglas on the set of Stanley Kubrick's 1960 movie, *Spartacus*, in which he played the title role.

Below: Douglas (right) co-starred as Doc Holliday alongside Burt Lancaster (left) in *Gunfight at the O.K. Corral* (1957).

Bob Dylan

Born Robert Allen Zimmerman
May 24, 1941
Duluth, Minnesota, USA

Evergreen and inscrutable, the hugely influential American singer-songwriter and rock musician, Bob Dylan, is one of the greats of the 20th century. He has been performing and touring for over 50 years.

Dylan first became an inspirational figure with his 1960s protest songs and the powerful lyrics of numbers such as *Blowin' in the Wind* and *The Times They Are a-Changin'* became anthems for the anti-war and civil rights movements of that era. His strong melodies and increasingly sophisticated lyrics came for a while to define the folk genre.

As a boy, Bob Dylan was influenced by contemporary blues, country and early rock and roll and his first albums were largely covers of existing folk, blues and gospel music. His first protest songs were in the melancholy style of his musical hero, Woody Guthrie, but he soon gained his own political and musical voice, notably on the 1964 album *The Times They Are a-Changin'.* His raw presentation of his own material was not to every taste, however and many of his early songs were initially hits for other people – *Blowin' in the Wind* for Peter, Paul and Mary in 1963 and *Mr. Tambourine Man* for The Byrds in 1965.

In 1965, Dylan shocked his more purist folk audience by choosing to perform with an electric rock band and was booed at the Newport Folk Festival. However, the intensity of his performance and the subtlety of the lyrics on his albums *Highway 61 Revisited* and *Blonde on Blonde*, reinforced by indecipherable and contradictory interviews, brought him celebrity status. The electric band (known simply as The Band) became a

permanent Dylan feature. The rock world was revolutionized by Dylan's new sound, a synthesis of his own varied styles with an overlay of British rock (Dylan and The Beatles met and worked together in 1964).

Dylan was showered with honors throughout the 1970s and 1980s – he was inducted into the Rock and Roll Hall of Fame in 1989 and given a Grammy Lifetime Achievement Award in 1991. His albums of the period were perhaps of variable quality. In 1988, however, he embarked on what became known as 'The Never-Ending Tour', a constant stream of live shows that continues to pull in capacity audiences. *Time Out of Mind* (1997), his first album of original material for seven years, received his strongest

reviews for years and three Grammy awards. In 2004, he was rated second in *Rolling Stone* magazine's 'Greatest Artists of All Time', stimulating a revival of interest in his music which was reinforced by the success of *Modern Times* (2006).

Academic critics have drawn attention to the cultural richness of Dylan's influences, literary as well as musical. In 2008, this was recognized with the award of a special Pulitzer citation for his profound impact on popular music and American culture.

Left: Dylan in concert, 1980.

Below: A young Bob with folk singer Joan Baez in 1965.

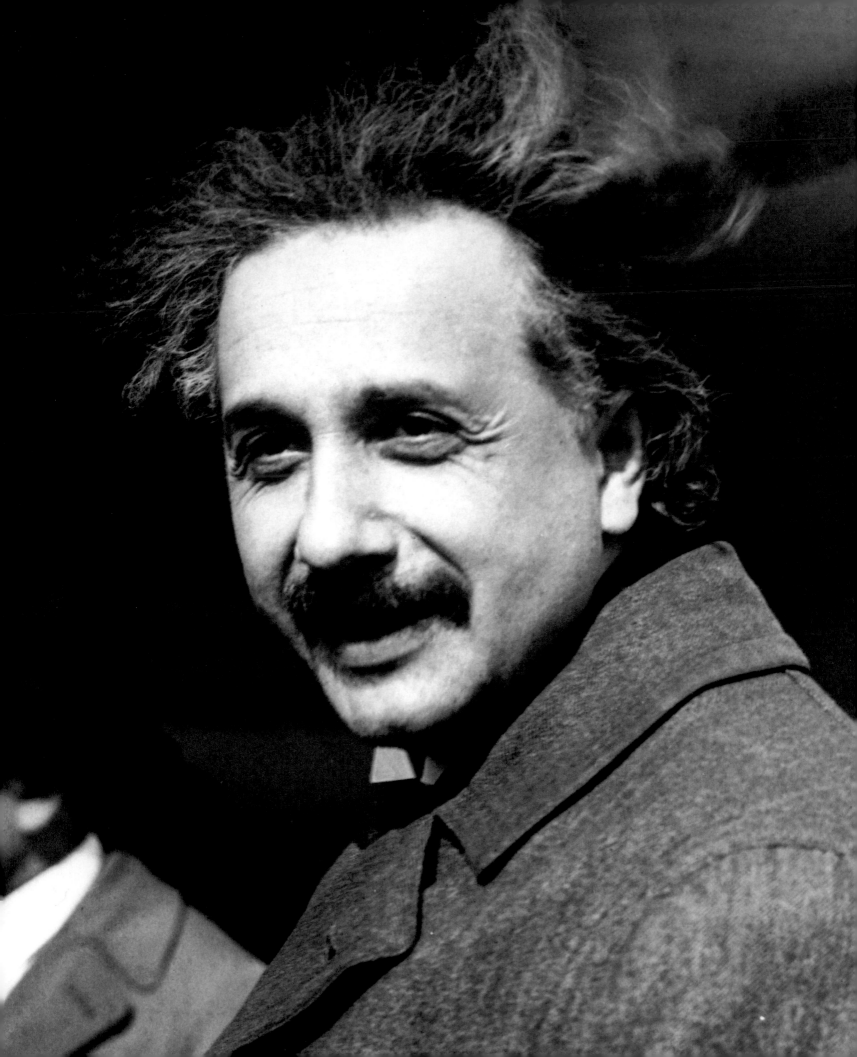

Albert Einstein

Born March 14, 1879
Ulm, Württemberg,
Germany

Died April 18, 1955
Princeton, New Jersey,
USA

Einstein stands alongside Galileo and Isaac Newton, as one of a handful of scientific thinkers, who have redefined our understanding of the universe. The German-born theoretical physicist and philosopher founded the concept of the 'space-time continuum' and is often described as the father of modern physics.

However, in his youth, Einstein's genius was not obvious. He struggled first to qualify for higher education and then to find a teaching post. While continuing to study, he finally landed a job in 1902 at the Swiss patent office – having already become a Swiss national – evaluating applications for electromagnetic devices.

In 1905, aged only 26, Einstein published four research papers, which came to be recognized as revolutionary in content and are known as the *Annus Mirabilis Papers*. Stimulated by apparent inconsistencies within current atomic and light-wave theory to take a new approach, Einstein sought to formulate new principles that might offer an underlying context for these puzzling phenomena, while remaining consistent with the established laws of physics. This new methodology has become the standard tool which defines modern theoretical physics.

His first new principle was that of special relativity, introduced in a paper on the electrodynamics of moving bodies, which postulated that the speed of light remains absolute, irrespective of the movement of the observer. He argued that as bodies approach the speed of light, they become shorter and heavier; this, in turn, led him to the view that energy (E) and mass (m) are two different aspects of the same thing. The resulting equation relating the two, $E = mc^2$, which many can cite, but few can explain, laid the basis for harnessing nuclear energy and the invention of the atom bomb.

Einstein's papers were so radical, that their significance was not immediately recognized. It was four more years before he was given a university post, a professorship at Zurich in 1909. In 1915, he generalized the theory of relativity to show its connection with gravitation, treating the gravitational force experienced by a body as a property of space and time, which he suggested was 'curved' by the presence of mass. The path of light and the motion of planets and stars are dictated by this curvature of space in the neighborhood of matter.

In 1919, when experimental data verified this theory, Einstein's name was finally made and in 1921, he received the Nobel Prize for Physics. He was lecturing in California when Hitler came to power in Germany in 1933 and as a Jew, wisely decided to stay in the USA. He became a US citizen and spent the rest of his life at the Institute for Advanced Study at Princeton, trying to formulate a unified field theory, a goal that still eludes physicists today. A pacifist, he was an active postwar supporter of nuclear disarmament, recognizing that the nuclear age had been launched by his theory of relativity.

Left and below: Einstein was arguably the best known scientist of the 20th century and his name is now a byword for exceptional intelligence.

Elizabeth II

Born Princess Elizabeth
Alexandra Mary of York
April 21, 1926
London, England

Iconic figures do not come any greater than the Queen of England, Elizabeth II. Queen since the age of 25, when she inherited the throne from her father George VI, she is constitutional monarch of the UK and 15 Commonwealth realms around the world, including Australia, New Zealand and Canada.

The eldest daughter of the Duke of York (the second son of King George V), Elizabeth was not immediately in line for the throne when she was born. Her father's elder brother Edward, Prince of Wales was expected to marry and have a family of his own, but only 11 months after becoming King in 1936 as Edward VIII, he abdicated. Elizabeth's father became King as George VI.

Princess Elizabeth was privately educated and served briefly in the army during World War II, before marrying her third cousin, Prince Philip of Greece in 1947. She acceded to the throne on the death of her father in 1952 and was crowned the following year in a glittering coronation ceremony.

Over 50 years later she remains one of the most well-respected monarchs in the world. She has reigned during an era of immense political and social change, presiding over it all with an aura of unflappable calm, and providing a reassuringly constant presence at the head of the nation. Eleven prime ministers have come and gone, beginning with Winston Churchill in 1952; Britain's colonial overseas territories have gradually gained independence; and she has ridden out increasingly strong calls for the introduction of a republic in Australia, once joking that she'd 'go quietly' if it was the will of the people.

The Queen is politically neutral and cannot publicly express an opinion on political matters. Her role as a constitutional monarch is largely ceremonial and titular, but she is the head of the armed forces, fount of justice and supreme governor of the Church of England.

One of the richest women in the world, she resides in palaces and castles (although most are held in trust), loves horses and owns a large private art collection. She is supported in her work by her family, her three sons, Charles, Prince of Wales, Andrew, Duke of York, Edward, Earl of Wessex and her daughter Anne, the Princess Royal. They represent Her Majesty at ceremonial events, helping to maintain the dignified public face of the monarchy.

One of the greatest changes of the Queen's reign has been the public attitude to royalty, which has become far less deferential. The private lives of her children, in particular, have been subject to intense press scrutiny and although the popularity of the monarchy dipped severely in 1997 when Diana, Princess of Wales died, it has since recovered. Queen Elizabeth, who is one of Britain's longest-reigning monarchs, has also proved to be one of the most popular and highly regarded.

Right: Cecil Beaton's iconic coronation portrait of Elizabeth II, 1953.

Below: The Queen opens parliament every year amid great pomp.

Overleaf: Queen Elizabeth II (3rd left), along with (left to right) Prince Harry, The Duke of York, The Duke of Edinburgh, The Earl of the Wessex and The Countess of Wessex wave to the crowd from a balcony at Buckingham Palace as part of the celebrations of the 60th anniversary of VE Day in London July 10, 2005.

Harrison Ford

Born July 13, 1942
Chicago, Illinois, USA

The ultimate rugged American box office draw, star of two of the most successful movie franchises of all time, the highest earning Hollywood actor ever – the superlatives come thick and fast where Harrison Ford is concerned.

However, Ford's career started slowly. Determined on an acting profession as soon as he left college, he moved to Los Angeles in 1964 to apply for a radio voice-over job. He played a number of bit-parts in film and television during the 1960s and early 1970s, including roles in *Ironside* and *The Virginian*, but became disenchanted with his progress and taught himself carpentry to support his young family.

In 1973, George Lucas cast him in a support role to Richard Dreyfuss in *American Graffiti*, but although the movie made Lucas's name, it still did not kick-start Ford's career. He played a couple of parts for Francis Ford Coppola, but was still doing his carpentry when, in 1975, Lucas asked him to read for a new project and finally cast him as Han Solo in the epoch-making sci-fi epic *Star Wars* (1977). Lucas himself said that he intended the movie, a classic struggle between good and evil, for a generation growing up without fairy tales and Ford's detached, but ultimately heroic character provided a welcome note of moral ambivalence.

Star Wars led to two follow-ups and also to Ford's next major outing, this time with the other great originator of movie blockbusters, Steven Spielberg. As Indiana Jones, in the riotous adventure escapade *Raiders of the Lost Ark* (1981), Ford reveled both in the intense action sequences – he performed many of his

own stunts – and in the knockabout humor. This, too, led to more films – *Indiana Jones and the Temple of Doom* (1984), *Indiana Jones and the Last Crusade* (1988), and *Indiana Jones and the Kingdom of the Crystal Skull* (2008).

After his first Indiana Jones outing, Ford's next major film, the bleak, futuristic *Blade Runner* (1982), was another gritty sci-fi style role. Any risk of typecasting was avoided by *Witness* (1985), in which his detective character joins an Amish community to protect a child witness to murder. The movie proved a sensitive exploration of different cultures and gained Ford an Oscar nomination. He reprised his portrayal of the troubled guy under abnormal pressure in *Presumed Innocent* (1990) and *The Fugitive* (1993), made his first romantic comedy with Melanie Griffith in *Working Girl* (1988) and subverted his own heroic image in the supernatural thriller *What Lies Beneath* (2000).

Ford returned to action movies in *Patriot Games* (1992), with Sean Bean and in *Air Force One* (1997), as the heroic US President saving the day. In 1997, he was ranked first in *Empire's list of* 'Top 100 Movie Stars of All Time'.

Having proved his versatility and starred in four of the ten top-grossing movies of all time, Ford has become choosier about his roles in the 21st century. He carefully guards his private life with his long-term girlfriend, the actress Calista Flockhart.

Above and overleaf: As Rick Deckard in Ridley Scott's *Blade Runner*, which Ford has called 'not one of my favorite films'.

Right: Ford's archetypal role, as gung-ho archeologist Indiana Jones, has made him the highest-earning Hollywood actor of all time.

Michael J. Fox

Born Michael Andrew Fox
June 9, 1961
Abbotsford, British
Columbia, Canada

Actor, voice-over artist and campaigner, Michael J. Fox is known above all for two long-running sitcoms, for his starring role in the *Back to the Future* trilogy and for his courageous revelation, in 1998, that he had been diagnosed with Parkinson's disease seven years earlier.

The son of a career soldier, during his childhood, Fox moved frequently around Canada with his family. His charmingly boyish face landed him his first acting job, playing a ten-year-old, when aged 15, in the CBC series *Leo and Me* (1976).

Roles in regional theater followed and in 1979, Fox dropped out of school and moved to Los Angeles. At first, he struggled and was all set to call it a day, when in 1981, he got the part of the aspiring, conservative, self-serving teenager, Alex P. Keaton, on the NBC sitcom *Family Ties* (1982–9). This won him three Emmy awards and made him one of the biggest stars of the 1980s, embodying the culture clash of the Reagan era in Alex's relations with his laid-back, liberal parents. The role was a defining one in a personal sense, too, as Michael met his future wife, Tracy Pollan, on set.

His effortless comic timing and classic 'boy-next-door' good looks earned him the part of time-traveling, guitar-playing Marty McFly in Steven Spielberg's hugely successful, light-hearted fantasy *Back to the Future* (1985). Unfortunately, this had the effect of typecasting him. He made a number of movies in the late 1980s in an effort to change career direction, but none of them won him the same acclaim. His most successful role was as a humane and horrified GI to Sean Penn's tough and depraved sergeant in Brian De Palma's bleak Vietnam War saga *Casualties of War*

(1989). His return in *Back to the Future 2* and *3* (1989 and 1990, shot back-to-back) was welcomed both by critics and the movie-going public and he added a new talent to his portfolio when he provided the narration for the Disney animal adventure remake *Homeward Bound: The Incredible Journey* (1993). More rewarding parts followed and in 1996, Fox signed for another sitcom, *Spin City*, as a fast-talking New York mayoral aide.

After announcing his diagnosis, Fox has continued to make public appearances, despite the shakes and tremors that are symptoms of Parkinson's, as part of his campaigning support for federally funded stem-cell research. He has also carried on acting, both doing voice-overs and taking

parts that reflect his own disabilities: he won an Emmy nomination for his four-episode role as a lung cancer patient in the television series *Boston Legal* and an Emmy award in 2009, for his abrasive paraplegic in the series *Rescue Me*. He founded the Michael J. Fox Foundation in 2000 to aid all avenues of research into the causes and treatment of neurological disorders.

Left: As Marty McFly, the time-traveling teenager in the *Back to the Future* movies.

Above: Fox's courageous struggle with Parkinson's disease, away from the silver screen, has earned him worldwide respect.

Aretha Franklin

Born Aretha Louise Franklin
March 25, 1942
Memphis, Tennessee, USA

The Queen of Soul, Aretha Franklin has enjoyed a long, distinguished and prolific musical career and is one of the most influential female artists of the 20th century. Renowned for her soul and R&B music, she is one of music's most versatile vocalists and has also released jazz, gospel, rock and pop numbers.

Aretha Franklin was born into a Baptist family and her father, the Reverend C.L. Franklin, encouraged his daughter's musical gifts. Aretha showed early promise as a dedicated pianist, with a powerful singing voice and her father allowed her to record her first album at the tender age of 14. Throughout her career, Franklin's music has shown a strong gospel influence, but by the time she signed with Colombia Records in 1960, her early hits were rooted more in jazz.

Although she enjoyed modest success in the early 1960s, it was not until she moved to Atlantic Records in 1967 that Franklin really hit her creative stride and was able to create her own distinctive sound. The 1967 blues ballad *I Never Loved a Man (The Way I Love You)* was quickly followed by Otis Redding's R&B number, *Respect*, the song that became Aretha's signature tune: it dominated the No. 1 spot for eight weeks and earned two Grammys in 1968.

Franklin went on to record music from several genres, as well as material she had co-written with her first husband and manager, Ted White, such as *Dr Feelgood* and *Since You've Been Gone (Sweet, Sweet Baby)*. With further hits, such as *I Say a Little Prayer* (1968), *Call Me* and *Spanish Harlem* (1971), Franklin had established herself as 'Soul Sister

Number 1' by the beginning of the 1970s. She had also notched up more million-selling records than any other woman in recording history.

Franklin continued recording at a prodigious rate during the 1970s, as well as performing live at show-stopping concerts, where she became known for her flamboyant costumes and occasionally erratic behavior. When her career seemed to be flagging, her role in *The Blues Brothers* movie (1980) and the release of her album *Who's Zoomin' Who* (1985) put Aretha back in the public eye and gave her a number of pop crossover hits. She worked with the best producers in the business – Quincy Jones, Luther Vandross and Curtis Mayfield – and during the 1980s recorded with artists as varied as the Eurythmics, Dizzy Gillespie and Carlos Santana. She had another big hit with her No. 1 duet with George Michael, *I Knew You Were Waiting for Me,* in 1987.

Showered with honors, musical, political, and charitable (including 18 Grammys), Aretha Franklin has performed at two presidential inaugurations, proof, if it were needed, of her position as a highly respected and admired American musical diva.

Left: Aretha gives a characteristically spirited performance at the inauguration of President Obama in January 2009.

Right: Franklin photographed backstage in 1979, a period when her career hit a low point, before reviving in the 1980s after her performance as Mrs Matt in the movie *The Blues Brothers*.

Clark Gable

Suave, sophisticated, dashing and with a thrilling whiff of danger, Clark Gable was one of the great box-office draws of 1930s and 1940s cinema. With his classic good looks and slightly world-weary air, he epitomized masculine glamour in the glory days of Hollywood and became one of cinema's first sex symbols.

Gable appeared as an extra in silent movies during the 1920s, but turned to the stage in 1927, at the urging of his friend, the actor and director, Lionel Barrymore. Offered a contract with MGM in 1930, he was rejected by Daryl F. Zanuck of Warner Brothers, because 'His ears are too big and he looks like an ape.' Nevertheless, Gable appeared in a succession of movies for MGM, graduating from supporting roles to romantic lead and played opposite some of Hollywood's legendary leading ladies, including Norma Shearer, Greta Garbo and Joan Crawford. Gable became immensely popular with the movie-going public, who never tired of his characteristic role as a charming rough diamond.

Frank Capra's *It Happened One Night* made Gable a true star and earned him an Oscar for Best Actor in 1934. He set female pulses racing as he removed his shirt to reveal a bare chest and apparently, caused a national downturn in sales of men's undershirts. Gable bared his manly torso again for his Oscar-nominated role as Fletcher Christian in *Mutiny on the Bounty* (1935) and went on to star in a series of popular romantic comedies, earning the nickname the 'King of Hollywood' in 1938.

However, the lasting image of Clark Gable is surely from *Gone with the Wind*, the epic 1939 movie that won ten Oscars and was Hollywood's first great blockbuster. Urged by his wife, Carole Lombard, to take the role of the raffish Rhett Butler, Gable gave one of his best performances, uttering the most memorable farewell in movie history, with his 'Frankly, my dear, I don't give a damn' to Vivien Leigh's Scarlett O'Hara.

After the death of Lombard, in 1942, in a plane crash, a grief-stricken Gable joined the Army Air Corps, serving for a short while with distinction, before returning to Hollywood. He never achieved quite the same level of fame after the war and several movies were panned by the critics. But his final role, in Arthur Miller's *The Misfits* (1961), in which he starred alongside Marilyn Monroe, recaptured some of the old magic: critics, as well as Gable himself, believed it was one of his best performances.

After Gable had performed all his own stunts in his last film, his already weak heart gave out and he suffered a heart attack, just two days after shooting ended. He died ten days later, leaving his fifth wife pregnant with the son he had always longed for.

Born William Clark Gable
February 1, 1901
Cadiz, Ohio, USA

Died November 16, 1960
Los Angeles, California,
USA

Left: Gable was the archetypal Hollywood idol during the golden years of the movie industry in the 1930s and 1940s.

Below: Gable in his most famous role, as Rhett Butler, with Vivien Leigh as Scarlett O'Hara, in *Gone with the Wind*.

Lady GaGa

Born Stefani Joanne Angelina Germanotta
March 28, 1986
New York, USA

Lady GaGa made a huge impact on the musical world from the moment she released her first record at the age of 19. With her striking, flamboyant appearance and distinctive voice, she is a rock star whose success is due partly to her ability to shock, as well as her considerable musical talent.

Lady GaGa's stage name is based on *Radio GaGa*, the hit single of another flamboyant group, Queen, and she takes much inspiration from the glam rock stars of the 1970s, such as David Bowie. Comparisons with Madonna are also inevitable, as they both seem to enjoy the mild sense of outrage that accompanies their performances. More pertinently, she has sold 15 million albums and 40 million singles in the space of two years.

Lady GaGa began life in an Italian-American family, growing up in New York, where she was a hard-working student who loved performing in school musicals. She studied for a short time at New York University's Tisch School of the Art, before dropping out to work on her own compositions. In 2005 her career began to take off when she was signed be Def Jam Recordings and recorded her first single, *Boys, Boys, Boys*. At the same time, she began working in burlesque shows, which has influenced her live performances and videos. In 2007 she played at the Lollapalooza music festival and her act, which incorporated electronic dance music and 1970s pop, brought her to the attention of Sony/ATV Music Publishing, who hired her to write songs for Britney Spears. Lady GaGa's own vocal talents were spotted by the singer-songwriter Akon, and he encouraged record executives to sign her as a recording artist.

Lady GaGa's debut album, *The Fame*, appeared in 2008 and featured the singles *Poker Face* and *Just Dance*. Drawing on many different influences, it was an immediate hit with both critics and fans around the world. She followed it with *The Fame Monster* in 2009, which explores the darker side of celebrity.

Provocative, original and often humorous videos accompany her hits, which feature scantily clad dancers and extravagant costumes, crafted with imagination and a vision that is refreshing in the world of music videos.

Lady GaGa is inventive, startlingly original and pushes the boundaries of the world of rock and pop. She dares to wear some incredible outfits, such as a PVC farthingale, a bubble-wrap minidress and a jacket adorned with Kermit the Frog heads. Rumors about her lifestyle surround her, but her global fame is the result of the hard work of a slightly eccentric, resolutely grounded individual determinedly focused on her career.

Left: A scantily clad Lady GaGa performs at London's O2 arena, 2010.

Right: An accomplished musician, GaGa sings at the Rainforest Funds 21st Birthday Concert at Carnegie Hall, 2010.

Overleaf: Lady Gaga performing on stage at the Nokia Theatre, Los Angeles, California in December 2009.

Mohandas Gandhi

Born Mohandas Karamchand
Gandhi
October 2, 1869
Porbandar, Gujerat, India

Died 30 January, 1948
New Delhi, India

Mahatma Gandhi, 'the enlightened one', was one of the most inspirational political leaders in history. He led the struggle for India's independence from Britain, during the first half of the 20th century, shunning the usual means of armed rebellion to advocate a policy of non-cooperation and non-violence. Gandhi's unusual protest methods inspired his followers in India and have since been adapted by political protesters and civil rights activists around the world.

Born in India, when the British Empire was at the height of its power, Gandhi trained as a lawyer in London and in 1893, began working for an Indian law firm in Durban, South Africa. Appalled by the inequalities in South African society, where Indian and black people were set apart from white people and treated as inferior races, Gandhi began to work to redress the problems of discrimination. He drew on many religious philosophies, as well as the work of writers such as Tolstoy and devised *satyagraha*, or passive resistance, as a means of righting wrongs. Faced with a public outcry against its repressive and brutal treatment of non-violent civilian protesters, Jan Smuts' government was eventually forced to concede to many of Gandhi's demands in 1914.

Gandhi returned to India in 1915 and was naturally drawn to the Indian National Congress, the political party that led the movement for Indian independence from British rule. He became the spiritual leader of the party and his policy of non-cooperation with the British included strikes and refusing to pay taxes and to respect colonial law. This was famously typified by his 240-mile 'March to the Sea' in 1930, in protest at the British salt tax. He was imprisoned several times by the British, as were thousands of his supporters, who boycotted British goods

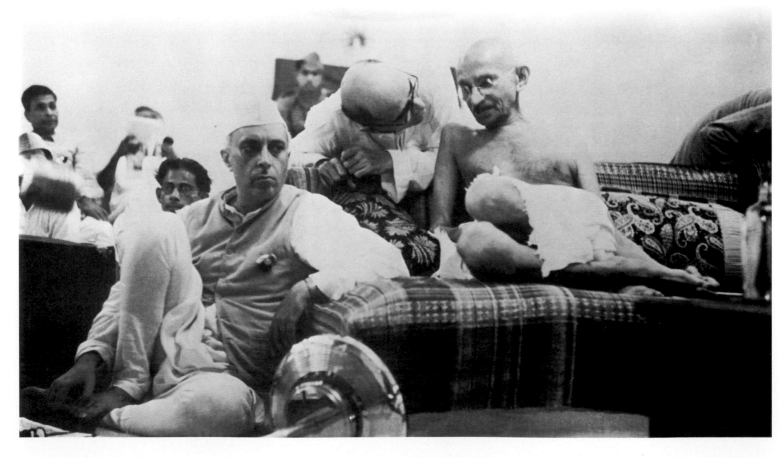

and institutions throughout India. His was not an easy path, but the action of a principled man, who profoundly believed that truth would transform society.

With the outbreak of World War II, Gandhi called for the British to 'Quit India,' intensifying the revolt against British rule. The British reacted forcefully, imprisoning him for two years, but they were obliged to respect his role as spiritual figurehead of India and released him in 1944. By 1945, it was clear that power would be transferred to the Indian nation. With Partition in 1947, the states of India and Pakistan were born.

Gandhi was assassinated by a Hindu extremist on January 30, 1948, just as he had launched his fast-to-death, in an attempt to end the communal violence that had broken out across the country between the Muslim and Hindu communities. A man of great moral courage, Gandhi is revered in India as the father of the nation and upheld, globally, as a model of what can be achieved by peaceful protest.

Left: Gandhi with the leaders of the All India Conference Committee in 1942, when they decided on their campaign of civil disobedience against British rule.

Right: Imprisonment only strengthened Gandhi's cause. This photograph shows him greeting his followers after his release from jail in 1931.

Judy Garland

Born Frances Ethel Gumm
June 10, 1922
Grand Rapids, Minnesota,
USA

Died June 22, 1969
London, England

Judy Garland, one of the great stars from the age of Hollywood musicals, spent her life chasing her own rainbows, after starring as Dorothy in the Hollywood blockbuster *The Wizard of Oz* in 1939. She was admired for her versatility as an actress and singer, but her professional triumphs were overshadowed by a messy and often unhappy private life.

Blessed with a powerful voice and the kind of perky star quality so popular in 1930s and 1940s cinema, Garland first appeared on stage at the age of three. The Gumm Sisters – Judy (then Frances, or 'Baby' as she was known) and her older sisters, Suzy and Jimmie, performed on the vaudeville circuit during the 1920s and early 1930s, before changing their name to the Garland Sisters. In 1935, Judy was signed by MGM and thrust into the studio system, where looks counted for everything. Short and self-conscious, she suffered years of insecurity about her appearance. Louis B. Mayer, a man not known for his tact, called her his 'little hunchback.'

She appeared in many juvenile roles, notably with Mickey Rooney, with whom she made nine successful films, such as *Babes in Arms* (1939). The pace of filming was relentless and the studio kept its young stars focused by plying them with amphetamines and barbiturates; Garland became addicted to them. Always keen to exploit a successful formula, MGM studio perhaps prolonged her youthful roles a little too long – aged 17, Garland was playing a 12-year-old in her most famous role as Dorothy in *The Wizard of Oz* and her costume incorporated a special corset to flatten her chest. Singing the song

that is forever associated with her, *Over the Rainbow*, she won a special juvenile Oscar for the role and became one of the brightest stars in the MGM firmament.

By the mid-1940s, Garland was finally being given adult roles. She appeared in a number of celebrated musicals such as *Meet Me in St. Louis* (1944) and *The Pirate* (1948), both directed by Vincente Minnelli, her second husband (and father of her eldest daughter, Liza Minnelli). Her outstanding success in *Easter Parade* (1948) was not immediately repeated and she was unable to complete several films, because of her dependence on prescription drugs. Her third husband, Sid Luft, arranged a concert tour of Britain in 1951 and Garland played to full houses, returning to Hollywood in 1954 to give an outstanding, Oscar-nominated performance in *A Star is Born*.

Garland was a legendary concert performer and is remembered as much for the critically acclaimed TV and concert performances she gave toward the end of her life, as for her movies. She died aged only 47, the pressure of the studio system, her personal insecurities and drug use having simply exhausted her.

Left: Garland in her most famous role, as Dorothy (with Toto the dog) in *The Wizard of Oz*.

Below: In her later career Garland was a formidable and very popular concert performer.

Bill Gates

Born William Henry Gates III
October 28, 1955
Seattle, Washington
State, USA

The brilliant founder of Microsoft is an unlikely icon, but Gates' invention of the MS-DOS computer operating system and subsequent computer software refined the personal computer and irrevocably changed the world we live in. It is perhaps truer to say that Microsoft and Windows, rather than Gates himself, are the real icons of the early 21st century.

An extremely bright child, fond of tinkering with early computers, Gates dropped out of Harvard after two years to pursue his passion for electronics and computer programming. He was more than just a technical buff – he foresaw that computers could be made to improve human lives, make businesses more efficient, operate machinery and relieve people of many humdrum chores.

He founded Microsoft with his school friend Paul Allen, an electronics expert, in 1975, working to produce programming code for Altair computers. At the time, computer programming was driven largely by amateurs as a hobby, but Gates persisted in his belief that software programmers should be paid for their work.

In the early years of Microsoft, Gates reviewed every line of code written by his staff. He was also a hardworking entrepreneur and spent much of his time negotiating deals with computer manufacturers, who needed efficient software to drive their machines. Gates could imagine a world with a computer on every desk and it was this goal that inspired him.

In 1980, Microsoft won the contract to produce an operating system for IBM's new personal computer and Gates designed an 'interface manager', which later became known as Windows. With the sale of the first Windows systems in 1985, Gates continued to pursue his vision of improving software, to make it easier and more enjoyable for everyone to use computers. He recruited the best technicians he could find and rewarded them well for their hours of hard, exacting work. He was aggressive both in positioning the Windows product and in drawing out the best from his staff.

Gates' success is legendary and made him, for many years, the world's richest person. In 2008, he stepped aside from his day job as head of Microsoft to concentrate on his charitable interests. He has become one of the most generous philanthropists in the world, using his enormous wealth to establish, along with his wife, the Bill and Melinda Gates Foundation. This has donated money to a long list of charities, including global health initiatives, education and agricultural projects around the world. Bill Gates has said that he wants to ensure 'that anyone who can reach a library can reach the internet', and the Foundation has made a special project of equipping public libraries in the United States with computers. Alongside his charitable work, he remains non-executive chairman of Microsoft.

Left: A young Bill Gates in 1983, on the brink of fame and fortune.

Right: Gates on the roof of Microsoft headquarters in Seattle, Washington, where there are some 30,000 employees.

Marvin Gaye

Born Marvin Pentz Gay Jr.
April 2, 1939
Washington DC, USA

Died April 1, 1984
Los Angeles, California,
USA

'The Prince of Soul', Marvin Gaye was one of Motown's greatest stars in the 1960s and 1970s, charming fans with his own brand of sensual soul music.

The son of a Pentecostal minister, Marvin spent his formative musical years with the gospel choirs of his father's church. As a teenager, he turned his back on gospel music and joined a band called the Marquees, which was promoted by the producer Harvey Fuqua and renamed the Moonglows. When Fuqua moved to Detroit to work with Berry Gordy at Motown, Gay (the 'e' was added in 1962 'because it sounded more professional') went with him, as a session drummer and vocalist.

In 1961, Gaye married Berry Gordy's sister, Anna and tied himself to Motown with more than just a paper contract. Gaye released a number of records in the early 1960s, with 1964's *How Sweet It Is (To Be Loved By You)* becoming an early signature song. With Berry Gordy keen to promote Gaye's image as a romantic lover, he performed with several female artists,

memorably Tammi Terrell. Their first album, *United* (1967), produced the classics *Ain't No Mountain High Enough* and *Your Precious Love*. At the same time, Gaye enjoyed international solo success, with one of his most enduring songs, *I Heard It Through the Grapevine* (1967).

Terrell's unexpected death from a brain tumor in 1970 plunged Gaye into depression, but he emerged in 1971 with the album *What's Going On*, which is considered one of his finest works. It was his most successful solo album. Yet Motown initially refused to release it, because – influenced by jazz and funk – it marked a new departure in Gaye's soul style. It was the first Motown album to concern itself with social issues and resonated with an American pubic torn apart by the Vietnam conflict.

Empowered by this success, on his next album, Gaye concentrated on a theme that preoccupied him for the rest of his life – sex. Overtly sensual, *Let's Get it On* (1973) was Gaye's best-selling album during his lifetime. He worked with Diana

Ross on his final duet album, *Diana & Marvin*, although, after the first recording session for it, they never actually worked in the same studio at the same time.

Meanwhile Gaye's personal life was disintegrating. Divorce and drug use affected his work at the end of the 1970s, although he bounced back with the amazingly successful *Midnight Love* in 1982, which featured the masterful *Sexual Healing*, his last hit, as its first track. Sadly, Gaye could not overcome his personal demons and he was shot dead by his father during a violent family argument, a tragic end for one of the legends of soul music.

Left: Marvin Gaye in concert, 1983.

Right: 'If you cannot find peace within yourself, you will never find it anywhere else', said Gaye, who was a troubled man. His mellow music belied his inner turmoil.

Left: Archie Leach from Bristol successfully reinvented himself as one of Hollywood's most debonair and amusing actors.

Right: One of cinema's most famous scenes from *North by Northwest*, in which the innocent Roger Thornhill (Grant) is pursued by a murderous biplane.

Overleaf: Cary Grant with Leslie Caron in a still from the 1964 movie *Father Goose*.

Cary Grant

Born Archibald Alexander
Leach
January 18, 1904
Bristol, England

Died November 29, 1986
Davenport, Iowa, USA

More than any other Hollywood actor, Cary Grant came to epitomize the suave, debonair male lead, displaying time and again an air of self-possession, charm and glamour that appealed to male and female fans alike. Painstakingly crafting an image that took over his life, he somehow remained an ageless, intelligent and humorous presence on the screen for nearly 40 years.

Grant's early life was not easy. His parents were poor and his mother was institutionalized when he was nine. The young Archie developed a love of the music hall and acquired odd jobs at local theaters, before joining the Bob Pender Comedy Troupe in 1918. At the end of their two-year American tour in 1922, Archie decided to stay in the USA. He struggled to find his feet before landing his first stage role five years later.

After modest success on Broadway, he moved to Hollywood in 1931. There, Paramount executives suggested he change his name and Cary Grant was born. He appeared as little more than eye candy in his early movies, opposite some of Paramount's female stars, such as Marlene Dietrich and Mae West – whose immortal line, 'Why don't you come up sometime and see me?', was directed at him.

It was after appearing in *Sylvia Scarlett* (1935) opposite Katharine Hepburn that Grant finally found his trademark role, as a charming, if slightly unreliable character, who could be relied on to win back the heroine. He starred in a succession of 'screwball' comedies, such as *Bringing Up Baby* (1938), *Only Angels Have Wings* (1939) and *The Philadelphia Story* (1940), bucking the trend by working outside the Hollywood studio system. Unlike many of his contemporaries, Grant was not afraid of physical comedy – he used his early training in Pender's Comedy Troupe to good effect, as he conducted perfectly timed prat-falls and slapstick.

Grant remained a prime box office draw, appearing in three of Alfred Hitchcock's great thrillers, *Notorious* (1946), *To Catch a Thief* (1955) and *North by Northwest* (1959). Although his later movies did not replicate the huge success of his earlier work, none of them actually lost money and Grant decided to retire gracefully in 1966, leaving his on-screen image untarnished. He was nominated twice for Oscars and received a special Academy Award for Lifetime Achievement in 1970.

Grant's personal life was a little more tumultuous than his professional career, with five marriages, four of them ending in divorce and rumors that he was bisexual. However, he rose above all the rumors, once saying enigmatically of his screen persona, 'I pretended to be somebody I wanted to be and finally, I became that person. Or he became me.'

Rolf Harris

Born March 30, 1930
Bassendean, Perth,
Western Australia

Painter, musician, composer and all-round entertainer, Rolf Harris has shone in an impressively wide range of fields and has come to be seen as an artist and educator in his own right.

Initially a television cartoonist, Harris went on to write and record enduring hit singles, such as *Sun Arise* (1962), which went to No. 2 in the UK charts, while also playing jazz and continuing to paint and draw. He has received many honors, including Commander of the Order of the British Empire (2006) and Member of the Order of Australia (1989), but perhaps the greatest was the commission to paint a portrait of Queen Elizabeth II for her 80th birthday in 2005.

A champion swimmer in his teens, Harris won a radio 'Amateur Hour' competition at the age of 18. After studying at the University of Western Australia, he arrived in England in 1952 to attend art school in Kennington, south London. Almost immediately he got involved in the early days of television, with a five-minute cartoon-drawing slot on the BBC.

In 1960, he returned to Perth to produce and star in a weekday children's program, as well as hosting his own weekly variety show. In the same year, he wrote and recorded his first hit single, the comic *Tie Me Kangaroo Down, Sport*, which has become his theme tune. Ever quick to recognize a trend, he wrote a special version of the song for The Beatles and performed it with them in 1963. *Sun Arise*, a more serious and lyrical aboriginal-style song, which introduced the didgeridoo (an indigenous Australian wind instrument) to western audiences, was beaten to the No. 1 spot by Elvis Presley in 1962.

In 1969, Harris had a surprise No. 1 UK hit – and his most successful single – with his re-recording of the old music hall tear-jerker *Two Little Boys*, about two friends who grow up to fight in the American Civil War. By 1973, he was sufficiently well established to perform the opening concert at the newly completed Sydney Opera House.

Television has remained his principal medium, however. He has appeared in a string of shows, initially as presenter and then in 1967, with *The Rolf Harris Show*, which remained a light entertainment staple throughout the 1970s and 1980s. He also starred in a number of television shows, such as *Rolf's Cartoon Club*, which focused more specifically on his artistic gifts. Many of his appearances were marked by him dashing off large pictures at speed and apparently effortlessly and at some point, asking the audience: 'Can you tell what it is yet?' Between 2001 and 2007, he presented *Rolf on Art*, in which he both introduced and imitated the work of notable artists. His portrait of Queen Elizabeth featured in a special edition of the program and in 2002, London's National Gallery featured an exhibition of his art.

Right: Rolf Harris has enjoyed an extraordinary 40-year career as a TV presenter, artist and musician. His appeal shows no sign of diminishing with his advancing years.

Below: Harris sketching a picture of Bambi for a TV audience in 1986.

Stephen Hawking

Born Stephen William Hawking
January 8, 1942
Oxford, England

The gifted theoretical physicist, Stephen Hawking, has achieved celebrity status by using the power of mathematics to advance our understanding of the universe.

Hawking has had a globally recognized scientific career, while his publications and public appearances have been hugely successful in explaining complex science to the general public. This is all the more astonishing, given that, since his early twenties, he has suffered from a type of motor neurone disease, which has progressively incapacitated him and talks only with the aid of a voice synthesizer.

After obtaining a first at the University of Oxford and a PhD at Cambridge, Hawking had his initial significant breakthrough, in collaboration with mathematician Roger Penrose, with their work on gravitational singularities – places in space, or time at which some quantity becomes infinite – in relation to Einstein's theory of general relativity. At the time, the most favored theory regarding the nature of the universe was the 'steady-state' theory, which saw it as having always existed. Penrose and Hawking built on Penrose's work in identifying the point inside a black hole where all mass shrinks to nothing – a 'singularity' – to argue that Einstein's concept of space/time must have an ending, in just such a final point.

Hawking then applied the argument to theories about the origins of the universe. He theorized that this had taken the form of a black hole in reverse and had begun as a singularity, an infinitesimal point containing the entire substance of the universe. This was the 'big-bang' theory, first proposed in the 1920s and now widely accepted as a result of Hawking's work. Since then, he has worked on identifying a theoretical link between general relativity, which deals with gravity and the other great scientific development of the earlier 20th century, quantum theory, which deals with miniscule events inside the atom. This is the unified field theory that Einstein unsuccessfully sought to define.

Recognition for Hawking's work was not slow in coming. In 1974, he was named a member of the prestigious UK scientific body, the Royal Society, at the unusually young age of 32. In 1979, he became Lucasian Professor of Mathematics at the University of Cambridge, a post he held for 30 years, until he retired in 2009. His book *A Brief History of Time: From the Big Bang to Black Holes* (1988) outlined his theories in terms intended to be comprehensible to non-scientists. The book spent over four years in the best-seller charts and Hawking followed it up in 2001, with *The Universe in a Nutshell*. He was made a Companion of Honour by Queen Elizabeth II in 1989 and was awarded the Presidential Medal of Freedom, the highest civilian honor in the US, in 2009.

Left: Hawking lecturing in Berlin, 2005.

Right: Stephen Hawking has overcome his considerable physical limitations to pursue a stellar career as the world's most famous theoretical physicist.

Jimi Hendrix

Born Johnny Allen Hendrix
November 27, 1942
Seattle, Washington, USA

Died September 18, 1970
London, England

Brilliant and original, the legendary rock musician, Jimi Hendrix, is often hailed as the greatest electric guitarist in the history of rock music. In his short life he established a riotous reputation, with his outrageous fashion sense and breathtakingly uncontrolled stage performances.

A self-taught guitarist, Hendrix initially worked as a backing musician, after two years in the US Army. By the time he moved to New York in 1964, he had played with some of the big names of the time, notably Sam Cooke, Little Richard and Wilson Pickett. In New York, he formed his first band, the Blue Flame. He moved to London in 1966, after meeting ex-Animals bassist Chas Chandler, who signed him as a performer and helped him to form a new band – the Jimi Hendrix Experience – with Noel Redding and Mitch Mitchell. Their first three singles, *Hey Joe*, *Stone Free* and *Purple Haze*, were all hits and their first album *Are You Experienced* (1967) became a blueprint for the potential of the electric guitar, which was recorded on four tracks and then mixed into mono. It made Hendrix a superstar and paved the way for other psychedelic and experimental rock acts.

Hendrix's stage performance began to develop at the same time. Booked as one of the opening acts on the Walker Brothers' farewell tour in March 1967, he set his guitar on fire at the end of his set and was warned by Rank Theatre management to tone down his suggestive stage act. The burning and smashing of a guitar became an integral part of the Hendrix act and a similar performance, at the Monterey International Pop Festival in California, was caught on film in 1968.

The next two albums, *Axis: Bold as Love* and the even more experimental *Electric Ladyland* made 1968 the band's most commercially successful year. But this was a high point. Hendrix came under pressure from Black Power supporters to form an all-black band, Chandler became frustrated with Hendrix's perfectionism and left and the Jimi Hendrix Experience finally broke up in 1969.

Hendrix's appearance with a scratch band at the Woodstock Festival in 1969 was a memorable one, it ended with his solo improvisation of *The Star-Spangled Banner*, now regarded as an iconic event of the era. In August 1970, with new manager Michael Jeffery, Hendrix opened his own recording studio, the Electric Lady Studios, in Greenwich Village, New York, which was designed especially for him; the aim was to offer a professional, yet relaxing recording environment to stimulate his creativity.

A European tour came first, however and a restless Hendrix cut some of his gigs short, earning booing and jeering at his final concert performance. Two weeks later, tragically young, he was dead, apparently from a drugs overdose, but in circumstances which remain mysterious.

Left: Hendrix pictured at the Monterey Pop Festival 1967, the day of his debut performance in North America.

Below: Hendrix gives a virtuoso performance in Boston in June 1970, shortly before his death.

Audrey Hepburn

Elegant, gamine and classically beautiful, Audrey Hepburn was a Hollywood goddess.

The star of over 25 movies, she became an actress almost by accident, but won an Oscar for her first Hollywood movie in 1954 and was nominated four more times over the course of her career.

Born in Belgium in 1929 and with Dutch, German and Bohemian relatives, Hepburn spoke five languages and spent her childhood shuttling between Europe and Britain. She trained first as a ballerina, but progressed to cabaret and revues and in 1951, to the movies in Britain. Cast as the eponymous *Gigi* in 1951, Hepburn's appearance on Broadway quite literally put her name in lights, where they remained for the rest of her career.

From Broadway, it was just a plane ride to Hollywood and in 1953, her first Hollywood movie, the charming and witty *Roman Holiday*, cast her opposite Gregory Peck and won her the Best Actress Oscar in 1954. Her signature style – restrained elegance, slightly unworldly, with a hint of promise – carried her through several films with some of Hollywood's finest actors and directors, such as Billy Wilder, John Huston, Humphrey Bogart and Cary Grant. A tall, slim woman, her natural grace and dancer's carriage were enhanced by the clothes of Givenchy, who dressed her for her next film, *Sabrina* (1954) and continued to design for her for the next

35 years. By the end of the 1950s, Hepburn was not only one of Hollywood's hottest stars but also, partly thanks to Givenchy, one of the most stylish women in the world.

She is probably best remembered, though, for her role as Holly Golightly in *Breakfast at Tiffany's* (1961), the film that came to epitomize her elfin grace, charm and sophistication. Naturally shy, Hepburn found it a challenge to portray such an extrovert character, but the role earned her another Oscar nomination. During the 1960s, she went on to star as Eliza Doolittle with Rex Harrison in *My Fair Lady* (with the vocals famously voiced by Marni Nixon), with Peter O'Toole in *How to Steal a Million* and with Albert Finney in *Two for the Road*.

Born Audrey Kathleen Ruston
May 4,1929
Ixelles, Belgium

Died January 20, 1993
Tolochenaz, Switzerland

Hepburn spent most of the 1970s, in semi-retirement, bringing up her two sons and working as a goodwill ambassador for UNICEF. Her wartime experiences, when she lived in the Netherlands under Nazi occupation, remained with her and she devoted a great deal of time to improving the lives of disadvantaged children around the world.

Her status as one of the world's most beautiful and elegant women seemed to mystify her, as she much preferred casual clothes and never felt that she was especially beautiful. Like it or not, the still of her in large hat with an oversized cigarette holder from *Breakfast at Tiffany's* remains a classic movie image and her 'little black dress' (by Givenchy) from the same film sold at auction in December 2006 for nearly one million dollars.

Right: Audrey Hepburn on the set of *Breakfast at Tiffany's*.

Left: Audrey Hepburn at the Studio de Boulogne, during the making of *How to Steal a Million* in Paris.

Above: Soon after becoming a UNICEF ambassador, Audrey Hepburn went on a mission to Ethiopia, where years of drought and civil strife had caused terrible famine.

Katharine Hepburn

Beautiful, elegant and witty, Katharine Hepburn was one of the few stars of Hollywood's golden age to enjoy a fruitful career that lasted for the whole of her long life. Fiercely independent both on and off screen, she established herself as one of the first actors to enjoy equality with her male counterparts. In addition, she won four Best Actor Oscars, more than any other star.

A Connecticut Yankee, she grew up in New England in a fiercely competitive family, excelling at sports and athletics, as well as demonstrating a formidable intelligence. While studying at Bryn Mawr College, she took up acting and when she left in 1928, embarked on a career in the theater. After appearing in numerous Broadway productions, she was spotted by a Hollywood scout and won a contract with RKO. Her first film, *A Bill of Divorcement* (1932) was directed by George Cukor, with whom Hepburn would make some of her best movies.

She was one of the tallest leading ladies of her day and this, coupled with her distinct feminist personality, meant that she often portrayed strong female characters, such as Jo in *Little Women* (1933) or the slightly androgynous lead in *Sylvia Scarlett* (1935). Hepburn was not afraid to challenge the studio bosses, aware of her own strengths as an actor and unwilling to take on a role just to fulfill superficial fashions. She won her first Oscar for *Morning Glory* in 1933, but after a string of flops, bought herself out of her RKO contract and returned to Broadway in 1939 to appear in *The Philadelphia Story*, which was written specifically for her. Nominated for the Best Actress Oscar, she played opposite Cary Grant and James Stewart in the movie version in 1940, which shows her at her best, full of charm, vivacity and rebelliousness.

In the 1940s she began her professional association with co-star Spencer Tracy in *Woman of the Year* (1942), the first of a series of likable movies they made

Born November 9, 1907
Hartford, Connecticut,
USA

Died June 29, 2003
Fenwick, Connecticut,
USA

together. In private, Tracy and Hepburn's 25-year relationship became one of Hollywood's worst-kept secrets.

Oscar-nominated for her role as the aloof spinster in *The African Queen* (1951) opposite Humphrey Bogart, Hepburn went on to play a succession of roles as slightly prickly women in *The Rainmaker* (1956) and *Suddenly, Last Summer* (1959). Finally, in 1967, eight nominations and 34 years after her first Oscar, she won another Academy Award for *Guess Who's Coming to Dinner*, her final appearance with Tracy, who died shortly after production. Her role as Eleanor of Aquitaine opposite Peter O'Toole in *The Lion in Winter* earned a third Oscar in 1968 and she won her fourth for the autumnal *On Golden Pond* with Henry Fonda (1981).

Hepburn's career was one of the most remarkable in Hollywood history and its longevity can be attributed to her enormous talent and vitality.

Left: Hepburn appeared alongside fellow Hollywood veteran Henry Fonda in *On Golden Pond*, in 1981.

Right: A publicity still of Katharine Hepburn at her most glamorous in the 1930s.

Overleaf: Hepburn and her co-stars, (left to right) Cary Grant, James Stewart and John Howard, in the 1940 film *The Philadelphia Story*.

Sir Edmund Hillary

Born	Edmund Percival Hillary July 20, 1919 Auckland, New Zealand
Died	January 11, 2008 Auckland, New Zealand

In May 1953, mountaineer and explorer Edmund Hillary, together with Sherpa Tenzing Norgay, became the first man to reach the summit of Mount Everest in the Himalayas, the highest mountain in the world.

A New Zealander by birth, Hillary first became interested in climbing during a school trip and made his first major climb in 1939, in the southern Alps. After studying at the University of Auckland, he took up beekeeping in the summer, in order to leave the winter months free for mountaineering.

During the 1940s, he made many climbs in New Zealand and then in Europe, establishing a reputation for daring, strength and reliability. He joined a reconnaissance expedition to Everest in 1951; the route from Tibet was blocked by China and the Nepalese permitted only one attempt a year on the alternative, southern, route. In 1952, Hillary was one of those invited by the Joint Himalayan Committee to join the planned official British expedition, under Sir John Hunt, in 1953.

A joint effort, comprising 400 people, the expedition set up its base camp – still today the starting point for Everest attempts – in March. By late May, it had worked its way up to the final camp, at 8,000 m (25,900 ft). Two climbers attempted the summit first, but had to turn back when an oxygen system failed and Hunt named Hillary and Tenzing as the next team to try. On May 29, they succeeded in reaching the summit – at 8,500 m (29,000 ft) one of the last untrodden places on earth. News of their success reached the UK on the day of Queen Elizabeth II's coronation and the group was stunned by the international reaction: Hillary was knighted only a week later, on June 6.

Further expeditions to the Himalayas followed in the 1950s and 1960s and Hillary also joined the Commonwealth Trans-Antarctic Expedition in 1958, leading the New Zealand section. His group was the first to reach the South Pole overland since Amundsen in 1911 and Scott in 1912. In 1974, he led an expedition by jet boat up the River Ganges to its source and in 1985, he accompanied astronaut Neil Armstrong on a flight that landed at the North Pole. In so doing, he became the first man to have stood at both poles and on top of the world.

After his Everest success, Hillary founded the Himalayan Trust, with the aim of helping the Sherpa people of Nepal and oversaw the building of schools and hospitals there. He was also honorary president of the American Himalayan Foundation, which focuses on the ecology of the region and of Mountain Wilderness, a worldwide body dedicated to mountain protection.

Left: A smiling Hillary with Sherpa Tenzing at base camp after their descent from Everest in June 1953.

Below: Hillary went on to explore the Antarctic with the Vivian Fuchs expedition in 1958.

Sir Alfred Hitchcock

Alfred Hitchcock was one of the world's greatest film directors and a master of the art of suspense-filled thrillers. He directed more than 50 films and is regarded by many as the best British filmmaker in cinematic history.

Hitchcock trained as a draftsman, and became interested in photography from an early age. From 1920 he used his graphic skills as a title-card designer for early silent movies. He was able to study film-making techniques and, by 1922, he was an assistant director. In 1924 he went to Germany, where the work of classic silent-movie directors F. W. Murnau and Fritz Lang proved extremely influential, particularly the Expressionist techniques that were fashionable at the time.

In 1926 Hitchcock released his first successful movie, the silent film, *The Lodger*, which incorporates themes of false accusation and intrigue that became staples of Hitchcock's art. He embraced sound technology as soon as it appeared, using it with great originality in his first sound movie, *Blackmail* (1929), emphasizing a woman's anxiety about a stabbing by distorting all the sound apart from the word 'knife'.

Hitchcock went on to make a series of extremely successful films in the UK, such as *The Man Who Knew Too Much* (1934), *The 39 Steps* (1935) and *The Lady Vanishes* (1938), constantly improving his narrative skills to produce tense thrillers that had audiences on the edges of their seats. Given this success, it was no surprise that in 1939, he accepted David O. Selznick's offer of a seven-year contract in Hollywood.

Somewhat ironically, Hitchcock's first Hollywood movie was *Rebecca*, the adaptation of an English novel, set in England and starring England's greatest actor, Laurence Olivier. However, Hitchcock appreciated the vastly superior financial resources of the American studios and the movie won the Academy Award for Best Picture in 1940. Hitchcock was nominated for the award as Best Director for this and four subsequent movies, but he never won.

Hitchcock produced his finest and most memorable movies between 1950 and 1960, when his reputation ensured that the Hollywood elite – Grace Kelly, Cary Grant, James Stewart, among others – competed to work with him. His movies were not only tautly structured, but they were also shot with great care and an attention to detail that enhanced the subtle nuances of the story. *Rear Window* (1954), *Vertigo* (1958), and *Psycho* (1960) are probably his most well-known masterpieces, each one haunting, intriguing and unforgettable.

Like Walt Disney, Hitchcock was one of the first film-makers to fully appreciate the importance of television, and from 1955 to 1965 he lugubriously hosted *Alfred Hitchcock Presents*, a popular series of dramas, thrillers, and mysteries. Hitchcock's screen presence, like his film directing, was always subtle and became a signature of his films. He delighted in making very brief cameo appearances in many of his movies, his portly silhouette appearing in the background as an extra.

Born	August 13, 1899 Leytonstone, England
Died	29 April, 1980 Bel Air, California, USA

Left: Thoughtful and intelligent, Hitchcock poses on his director's chair, 1954.

Right: Hitchcock with Tippi Hedron, star of *The Birds*, 1963.

MR. HITCHCOCK

Michael Jackson

Born Michael Joseph Jackson
August 29, 1958
Gary, Indiana, USA

Died June 25, 2009
Los Angeles, California,
USA

Known as the King of Pop, Michael Jackson was quite simply the most successful entertainer of all time.

Jackson was the world's biggest-selling solo artist, with sales in excess of 750 million albums. His undeniable vocal talent was complemented by a distinctive musical style, superbly choreographed dance moves and a private life that can best be described as idiosyncratic. The combination of his gentle and childlike public persona, enormous personal wealth and all-conquering musical talent made him one of the great musical icons of the late 20th and early 21st centuries.

The eighth child of ten, Jackson made his first stage appearance in 1964, alongside his elder brothers and two years later, became a permanent member of the Jackson 5. Aggressively promoted by their father, Joe, the band were signed by the Motown label in 1969. During the early 1970s, their energetic and appealing performances made them one of pop's biggest acts. Crowds of screaming girls – as many white as black – accompanied every public appearance. Young Michael stood out from his brothers, partly because of his age and size, but more importantly, because of his enormous talent.

The release of the solo album *Off the Wall,* in 1979, signaled the beginning of a phenomenal solo career. When *Thriller* was released in 1982, rumors of Jackson's personal strangeness merely fueled the fans' ardor. Critics and peers, however, united in their praise of his vocal skills and mastery of the pop genre.

Thriller was marked by the release of what has become one of the most famous music videos ever. It was one of the first to combine a complex storyline, fabulous and much-copied choreography and amazing special effects to produce an innovative and highly influential film. The man who gave the world unique dance moves, such as the moonwalk, continued to dazzle audiences throughout the 1980s and the album *Bad*, released in 1986, generated five No. 1 singles.

By the early 1990s, Jackson's private life had begun to dominate the headlines. Allegations of plastic surgery, skin lightening and close relationships with young boys at Neverland – his ranch retreat-cum-personal theme park in California – clouded his reputation and attracted widespread ridicule. His two short-lived marriages (firstly to Lisa Marie Presley, the only daughter of Elvis Presley and secondly to Debbie Rowe, a nurse) were regarded as shams. Allegations of child abuse, in 1994 and again in 2005, threatened to overwhelm both his personal and professional standing and he was driven to near bankruptcy.

Nevertheless, Jackson's sudden and premature death, in June 2009, was a huge shock to millions of fans around the world, who had remained loyal to him throughout the tribulations and provoked an outpouring of grief for an unassailable talent. The bizarre rumors that had surrounded his lifestyle contributed to his status as a musical icon almost as much as the music itself.

Left: Michael Jackson dancing during his performance in Munich's Olympic stadium on June 27, 1999.

Below: A young Michael Jackson talking on the phone in April 1971.

Overleaf: Jackson at the height of his fame, during his 'Bad' tour, 1987.

Sir Peter Jackson

Born Peter Robert Jackson
October 31, 1961
Pukerua Bay, New
Zealand

Peter Jackson seemed an improbable director to film J.R.R. Tolkien's epic fantasy series *The Lord of the Rings*. But in the event, his vision and commitment proved inspired and the result was a barn-storming Oscar-laden success.

Born in New Zealand, Jackson became a fan of film-maker Ray Harryhausen's mix of animation and live action and of the television series *Thunderbirds*. He began making short films, learning on the job and his first feature, the 1987 horror comedy *Bad Taste* – a team effort with friends, shot largely at weekends – gained a cult following. When two more gore-infested movies followed – *Meet the Feebles* (1989), shot with Muppet-style puppets, and the zombie horror *Braindead* (1992) – Jackson's style seemed established.

The lurid black comedy *Heavenly Creatures* (1994), however, proved otherwise. Based on real events, it is a chilling tale of two teenage girls, who concoct a shared fantasy world that turns murderous. The movie launched Kate Winslet's career, gained Jackson an Oscar nomination for Best Screenplay and led to his first big budget Hollywood film, *The Frighteners* (1996), starring Michael J. Fox.

By then, Jackson had already begun negotiations for the film rights to the supposedly unfilmable *The Lord of the Rings*, with the aim of making a serious fantasy film, which would exploit the new developments in computer-generated imagery (CGI). The deal-making proved tortuous, with the trilogy reduced first to two films and then to one. Finally, in 1998, a new backer gave Jackson the go-ahead to shoot all three films back-to-back in his native New Zealand.

The project involved planning on an epic scale: 150 different locations were used; the New Zealand army helped to build Hobbiton months before shooting, so that the planting would be mature; and a premier cast spent over a year on location, forming a strong bond in the process. Marketing began 18 months before the release of the first film, *The Fellowship of the Ring*, in December 2001; the online promotional trailer registered 1.7 million download hits in its first 24 hours. The film's pulsing soundtrack and gritty realism, together with its epic theme of good versus evil, chimed with a public facing overseas war and domestic terrorism and won four Oscars. Its two successors were released in the following two years, with the final installment, *The Return of the King* (2003), winning all the 11 Oscars for which it was nominated, an extraordinary achievement.

Jackson has followed this up with a successful version of *King Kong* (2005), for which Universal paid him a record upfront salary of $20 million. An adaptation of the best-selling novel *The Lovely Bones* (2009) was less well received. Undaunted, he is now working on a two-part adaptation of Tolkien's first novel, *The Hobbit*. In 2010, he was knighted by Queen Elizabeth II.

Right: Peter Jackson brandishes one of the 11 Oscars won in 2004 for *The Return of the King*.

Below: Jackson was apparently inspired to become a film director when he watched the 1933 version of *King Kong* as a child. He released his version in 2005, pocketing the highest advance ever paid to a film director.

Sir Elton John

Born Reginald Kenneth Dwight
March 25, 1947
Pinner, Middlesex,
England

A flamboyant and durable singer, songwriter and pianist, Elton John has sold more than 250 million records in his 40-year career.

Young Reginald Dwight (he formally took the name Elton Hercules John in 1972) was a talented pianist from an early age. He won a junior scholarship to London's Royal Academy of Music at the age of 11 and began his musical career as a pub pianist. His first band, Bluesology, toured with some big names, including Long John Baldry and in 1967, he began a song-writing partnership with lyricist Bernie Taupin that still continues today. He launched his solo singing career with the album *Empty Sky* (1969); a follow-up, *Elton John* (1970), was his first solo hit and established his music as a successful blend of pop and rock. A stream of well-received albums followed and by 1972, he had formed the Elton John Band, which performed both as instrumental players and as strong backing vocalists.

Much of John's commercial success in the 1970s was due to his impassioned performances, extravagant piano style and famous stage image, complete

with outrageous costumes and monster glasses. Perhaps the hottest act in the rock world, he filled venues worldwide. Seven albums in a row reached the UK No. 1 slot, between 1972 and 1975 and produced a string of hit singles, like *Rocket Man*, while his memorable duet with Kiki Dee, *Don't Go Breaking My Heart*, topped both US and the UK charts in 1976.

A period in the doldrums followed, with the occasional hit and much personal upheaval. This included a brief marriage to an old friend in 1984, which ended four years later when John finally confirmed that he was gay. At about the same time, he underwent throat surgery, which resulted in the loss of his famous falsetto voice.

A No. 1 hit in 1990 with *Sacrifice* saw the start of a happier and more productive period. The songs John wrote jointly with Tim Rice for the Disney film *The Lion King* (1994) gained three Oscar nominations, with the Best Song award going to *Can You Feel the Love Tonight*. John also founded the Elton John AIDS Foundation in 1992 and has dedicated a proportion of his earnings to AIDS-related research ever since. Personal happiness arrived in 1993, when he met David Furnish, now his civil partner. In September 1997, John performed a special version of his single *Candle in the Wind* to emotive effect at the funeral of Diana, Princess of Wales. The recorded version has sold over 37 million copies and a knighthood followed in 1998.

Elton John's song-writing success peaked with the music for the runaway West End and Broadway success, *Billy Elliot the Musical* (2005). John continues to tour to huge acclaim, celebrating his 60th birthday in 2007 with a record-breaking 60th concert at Madison Square Garden, New York.

Left: Elton and his writing partner Bernie Taupin, 1971. Taupin has penned the lyrics for most of Elton's hits.

Far left: Elton began his career as a pub pianist at the age of 15. Half a century later, his presence fills arenas all over the world.

Michael Jordan

Born Michael Jeffrey Jordan
February 17, 1963
Brooklyn, New York, USA

Professional basketball player, phenomenal athlete and shrewd businessman, Michael Jordan is generally regarded as the greatest basketball player of all time. He raised the National Basketball Association to worldwide superstardom in the 1980s and 1990s.

Born in Brooklyn, Jordan moved as a child to North Carolina with his family. At high school, he tried out for the basketball team, but at 5 ft 11 in (1.8 m) he was told he was too short. However, the next year he grew 4 in (10 cm) and made the team, earning a basketball scholarship in 1981 to the University of North Carolina at Chapel Hill. In both 1983 and 1984, he was selected for the NCAA All-American First Team. He won a gold medal in the 1984 Olympics in Los Angeles and left college a year early to join the Chicago Bulls.

Jordan won Rookie of the Year Award in his first season with the Bulls and immediately established himself with fans everywhere. In his first game at Madison Square Garden in New York, against the New York Knicks, he received a standing ovation. Attendances, both at home in the Chicago Stadium and on the road, rose dramatically and just a month into his professional career, Jordan was featured on the cover of *Sports Illustrated* under the headline 'A Star is Born.' He played a versatile game and was known for his power and agility on court, his leadership abilities, his prolific scoring and his extraordinary leaps to the basket, which earned him the nicknames 'Air Jordan' and 'His Airness'. Sponsorship offers followed and Jordan became known for his astute product endorsements – Air Jordan Nike trainers still remain popular today.

From the 1987–8 season onward, Jordan notched up a long sequence of record-breaking achievements. He was the first player since Wilt Chamberlin to score 3,000 points in a single season. In 1988, he received the NBA Most Valuable Player Award, a feat repeated in 1991, 1992, 1996 and 1998. The Bulls won their first NBA championship in 1991 and won it again in 1992 and 1993, securing a 'three-peat.'

Though traumatized by the murder of his father in July 1993, when he retired temporarily from the game, Jordan returned strongly in 1995 to help the Bulls win the championship again. He also starred in the mixed live action/animation film *Space Jam* (1996). In the following season, he started all 82 games – the Bulls won 72 of them and took the championship yet again – and averaged 30.4 points.

Jordan retired again in 1999, becoming part-owner of the Washington Wizards. He returned to play for a couple of seasons, but retired for good in 2003. In 2009, he was named greatest North American athlete of the 20th century by US cable TV network ESPN and was inducted into the Basketball Hall of Fame.

Left and right: Michael Jordan enjoyed a stunning career as the most famous and successful basketball player in the world, gaining lucrative sponsorships from some of the world's major brands.

Gene Kelly

The foremost dancer and choreographer in Hollywood during the 1940s and 1950s, Gene Kelly was an innovative and athletic performer who mastered a number of different dance styles.

Born in Pittsburgh, Kelly was taken to dance classes by his mother from the age of eight, although he and his brother hated it, partly because of the unwanted attention it attracted from neighborhood bullies. However, he persevered as he grew older and the Kelly family opened a dance studio in Pittsburgh in 1930. Kelly pursued a dual career, studying economics and law at university, while teaching at the dance school. Eventually he dropped out of law school to devote his energies to dance full time and in 1937 he moved to New York to work as a choreographer.

Kelly gradually established a reputation on Broadway and in 1939 won his first leading role in Rodgers and Hart's *Pal Joey*. His screen test in 1935 had been unsuccessful, but his undoubted talents attracted the attention of Hollywood and he signed a seven-year contract with David O. Selznick in 1941. He appeared with Judy Garland in *For Me and My Girl* (1942) and quickly established himself as a handsome leading actor. The following year he choreographed his own routines in *Thousands Cheer* and by 1945, MGM allowed him to devise all the dance routines in *Anchors Away* (the first of three films in which he was paired with Frank Sinatra). The two musicals for which Kelly is best remembered are *An American in Paris* (1951) and *Singin' in the Rain*

(1952); for the first, Kelly was co-director, leading man and choreographer. Both movies won Oscars and Kelly himself was awarded a Special Academy Award in 1951, recognizing his exceptional talents as a dancer and choreographer.

Kelly worked hard for his success and was well known for rehearsing his routines long after everyone else had gone home. His athletic routines were appealing, technically brilliant and imaginative and in his later career he strove to promote dancing as a man's game, emphasizing the link between athletics and dance. He also tried to bring dance into the real world, by choosing costumes and scenarios that were relevant to the average cinemagoer. Unlike Fred Astaire who performed sublime routings in top hat and tails, Kelly wore everyday clothes and would dance through streets, puddles, with mops and on roller skates. He used a wide variety of dance styles, and, as he said himself, 'I don't have a name for my style of dancing...It's certainly hybrid...I've borrowed from the modern dance, from the classical and certainly from the American folk dance – tap-dancing, jitterbugging...But I have tried to develop a style which is indigenous to the environment in which I was reared.'

Born Eugene Curran Kelly
August 23, 1912
Pittsburgh, Pennsylvania

Died February 2, 1996
Beverly Hills, California

Left: *Singin' in the Rain*, 1952, Kelly's most famous role.

Below: Kelly, as Jerry Mulligan dancing with Leslie Caron as Lise Bouvier in the 1951 movie, *An American in Paris*.

Grace Kelly

Born Grace Patricia Kelly
November 12, 1929
Philadelphia,
Pennsylvania, USA

Died September 14, 1982
Monaco

An exquisitely beautiful actress, who brought genuine glamour and style to her film-making, Grace Kelly, passed briefly, but memorably, through Hollywood to become a real-life princess.

Her father, the son of Irish immigrants, was an athlete and self-made millionaire and Kelly was brought up in high Philadelphia style. She attended the prestigious American Academy of Dramatic Arts in New York, where her graduation performance was in *The Philadelphia Story*. Her first acting roles were on stage and she made her Broadway debut in Strindberg's *The Father*, alongside Raymond Massey. She was Gary Cooper's choice for her first starring role, as his demure Quaker bride in *High Noon* (1952). As with many of her later films, rumors were rife of an on-set affair between Kelly and her leading man.

Meanwhile, Kelly had landed a seven-year contract with MGM, her first film being the supporting role in *Mogambo* (1953), with Clark Gable and Ava Gardner, for which she won an Oscar nomination. Oddly, her one Oscar-winning role was a non-glamorous one in *The Country Girl* (1954), where she played the long-suffering wife of alcoholic has-been actor, Bing Crosby.
In 1956, she played the haughty rich girl in the delightful MGM musical *High Society* (1956), an update of *The Philadelphia Story*.

But it was the pairing with director Alfred Hitchcock that made Kelly truly memorable. One of a series of signature blonde actresses with whom Hitchcock did some of his best work, Kelly played the beautiful, vulnerable, yet ambiguous heroine in *Dial M for Murder* (1954), the victim of husband Ray Milland's devious plotting. Next, Hitchcock cast her with James Stewart in the gripping *Rear Window* (1954). Stewart played the part of a news photographer encased in plaster, who risks both his own and his girlfriend's (Kelly) life investigating what he believes to be a murder. Kelly's final outing for Hitchcock was yet another alluring and equivocal role, flirting with and entrapping Cary Grant's retired jewel thief in the romantic comedy *To Catch a Thief* (1956). The chemistry between the stars was such that Kelly's future husband did his best to bury the finished film.

In 1955, Kelly met Prince Rainier of Monaco when she led the US delegation at the Cannes Film Festival. She married him a year later in a sumptuous ceremony in Monaco Cathedral. From then on she devoted her life to creating the role of gracious and immaculate princess consort. The occasional offers of a starring role – as the lead in Hitchcock's *Marnie* in 1962, for instance – were firmly rejected. In 1982, at the age of 52, Kelly had a stroke at the wheel of her car on a precipitous mountain road and died from the injuries sustained in the crash.

Right: With her classically beautiful features, Grace Kelly epitomized the Hollywood goddess.

Left: Kelly's longest role was as princess consort to her husband, Prince Rainier of Monaco, after their 1955 marriage, in which old world royalty merged with new world glamour.

John F. Kennedy

Born John Fitzgerald Kennedy
May 29, 1917
Brookline, Massachusetts,
USA

Died November 22, 1963
Dallas, Texas, USA

JFK – reforming Democratic politician and American statesman, 35th president of the USA and assassination victim – is one of the totemic figures of the 20th century.

Kennedy was no stranger to power. His multi-millionaire father had been a supporter of Roosevelt's New Deal to rescue the US from the Depression and served as the US ambassador in London. A brilliant student, JFK studied at both Harvard and London universities and was decorated for his wartime service as a torpedo boat commander in the Pacific. His already troublesome back was further damaged in action and though he underwent several spine operations in the 1950s, he spent much of the rest of his life in pain.

Returning to a political career, he entered the House of Representatives in 1947 and the Senate in 1952. In 1953, he married Jacqueline Lee Bouvier, who was to become as iconic in her own right as her famous husband. By 1956, he was already sufficiently well established to come second in the nominations for presidential running mate to Adlai Stevenson, who then lost the election to Eisenhower.

Declaring his intention to run for president himself in January 1960, Kennedy established himself as a candidate with broad popular appeal, despite the suspicion among conservative Protestants of his Catholicism. The series of televised debates between JFK and his republican rival, Richard 'Tricky Dicky' Nixon, which Kennedy, the more relaxed and authoritative performer, was deemed to have won, marked a milestone moment when TV was recognized as a dominant force in politics.

Defeating Nixon to become the second youngest and first Catholic president, Kennedy entered the White House on a wave of popular enthusiasm and his 1,000-day tenure came to be dubbed 'the Camelot years.' His inspiring inaugural address ('Ask not what your country can do for you; ask what you can do for your country') struck a note of international idealism that chimed well with the new decade.

Even so, the election was one of the closest in history and JFK's liberal domestic 'new frontier' policies, involving tax and social reforms and further racial integration, were significantly shackled by a conservative Congress. The abortive Bay of Pigs invasion of Cuba in 1961, planned by his predecessor to depose Castro, was undoubtedly a factor in Castro's agreement to a Soviet missile site in Cuba. This, in turn, precipitated the Cuban Missile Crisis of October 1962, which brought the world to the brink of nuclear confrontation.

Having established cordial relations with USSR premier Khrushchev, however, JFK achieved a nuclear test-ban treaty with him and the UK in 1963. His murder in Dallas in November 1963, ostensibly by a lone assassin, Lee Harvey Oswald, remains the subject of debate and many conspiracy theories.

Left: Kennedy was an impassioned public speaker, who inspired audiences.

Right: The Kennedys in the motorcade in Dallas minutes before the president's assassination, November 22, 1963.

Overleaf: President John F. Kennedy making his inauguration speech from the balcony of the White House in Washington, DC.

Martin Luther King Jr.

Born January 15, 1929
Atlanta, Georgia, USA

Died April 4, 1968
Memphis, Tennessee, USA

Martin Luther King's fiery oratory inspired both black people and white people to believe that the world could be a better place, where people of all beliefs and colors could live together peacefully and equally.

The son of a Baptist pastor, Martin Luther King followed his father into the church and assumed his first ministry in 1955, in Montgomery, Alabama, in the heart of the segregated southern states of the USA. He immediately worked with the leaders of the Montgomery bus boycott, when black people boycotted the local buses for over a year to protest against segregation. Eventually the bus company was driven to near bankruptcy and the US Supreme Court was forced to declare segregation on the Montgomery buses illegal.

King went on to found the Southern Leadership Christian Conference (SCLC) in 1957, to protest further against discrimination and advance the civil rights cause. Unlike many of his radical colleagues, King admired the ideals of Gandhi and advocated nonviolent protest to force the government to accept African-American demands for equality. He believed that media coverage of well-organized protests against the South's discriminatory laws would politicize Americans and push the civil rights issue to the top of the political agenda.

King's oratory, organization and righteous moral anger galvanized public opinion. Mass protests against discrimination in Birmingham, Alabama, throughout 1963 led to thousands of arrests and violent clashes between protesters and police, as well as between the white population and civil rights activists. Attacked many times himself, King was arrested and jailed for his part in the protest. Undeterred, he led the largest of the civil rights protests, the March on Washington in August 1963, when he faced a crowd of 250,000 and inspired listeners around the world with his 'I have a dream' speech. He articulated a simple vision of freedom and justice for all and his actions led directly to the landmark 1964 Civil Rights Act, which outlawed racial segregation. The Nobel Peace Prize in 1964 signaled international recognition for King's work.

The protests continued, culminating in the violent Selma to Montgomery marches in 1965, when King led the campaign for black voter registration. His message of peaceful protest had proven effective, but the pace of change was too slow for many and the civil rights movement lost its unity. King's dream ended abruptly when he was shot in Memphis, Tennessee, in 1968 and the riots that shook several American cities in the aftermath of his death were a tribute to the esteem in which he was held. Black America felt it had lost its protector.

However, King's work for the civil rights movement of America was a lasting legacy. He is still revered as a formidable human rights activist and a courageous man who overcame enormous prejudice to better the lot of humanity.

Right and below: Throughout his career, Martin Luther King was renowned for his oratory, which managed to be both inspirational and measured. He urged black people to stand up and protest peacefully for their civil rights, while warning against violent action.

Led Zeppelin

Formed 1968
Disbanded 1980

Members John Bonham 1948–80
John Paul Jones 1946–present
Jimmy Page 1944–present
Robert Plant 1948–present

Led Zeppelin were the most successful British rock band of the 1970s.

The band emerged in the dying days of the 1960s, from the demise of the Yardbirds. Guitarist Jimmy Page recruited John Paul Jones, drummer John Bonham and vocalist Robert Plant to his band, the New Yardbirds, in 1968. They recorded their first album in a record 30 hours and changed the band's name to Led Zeppelin, at the suggestion of The Who's Keith Moon.

Embarking on a tour of the US, they were delighted when their first album, *Led Zeppelin* (1969), reached the Billboard Top 10 within just two months. Led Zeppelin's sound was like no other at the time, with carefully arranged screaming guitar riffs, distorted amplification and amazingly loud vocals. It was the beginning of heavy metal. But the band were not just guitar thrashers – they also had a sensitive side, displayed to great effect in their most famous song, *Stairway to Heaven* (1971), which builds slowly from almost madrigal-like melodies to a full-blown hard rock-fest. Both Page and Plant were heavily influenced by blues music and both had an interest in the occult and mythology, which showed itself in mystical (and occasionally mystifying) lyrics.

The release of *Led Zeppelin II* was an even greater success than their debut album, reaching the No. 1 chart position in both the UK and US. It was recorded in a year packed with concert tours – four in the US and four in Britain. The album's first track, *Whole Lotta Love*, was a massive hit in the US, but the band generally resisted issuing singles, believing that each album was an entire musical entity and a listening experience in itself.

In 1973, the band's tour of the US broke box office records set by The Beatles and two years later, with concert and record sales from their albums at a new high, they were officially the most popular rock band in the world. In the mid-1970s, Led Zeppelin came to epitomize rock star excess, traveling by a private jet nicknamed 'The Starship' and trashing hotels.

After the formation of their record label Swan Song, the band released their first double album, *Physical Graffiti*, in 1975, which became their biggest selling record and a critical success. With *Presence* (1976), Led Zeppelin abandoned their mild flirtation with Celtic and folk influences to return to heavy rock and *In Through the Out Door* was the group's last album, recorded in 1978. Their next tour in 1980 was abandoned, when John Bonham died and the group reluctantly decided to split. Page and Plant have since had successful solo careers, but nothing has recaptured the sheer flamboyance and hard rocking glory of Led Zeppelin at the peak of their career.

Above: Robert Plant, John Bonham and Jimmy Page in 1970, after receiving the *Melody Maker* pop poll award for the best British group.

Right: Plant on stage in New York, 1988.

Bruce Lee

Born Lee Jun Fan
November 27, 1940
San Francisco, California,
USA

Died July 20, 1973
Hong Kong

Bruce Lee almost single-handedly revived the West's interest in martial arts during the 1960s and 1970s, with a string of Hong Kong-and-Hollywood-produced action movies. A diminutive dynamo, Lee moved with lightning speed, flying through the air to land punches and kicks precisely where they were needed.

Lee was born in San Francisco, but grew up in Hong Kong. Life was not entirely easy for the young Lee on the gang-filled streets of postwar Hong Kong: though his family was wealthy, Lee was constantly involved in street fights. This inspired him to take up martial arts and from the age of 13, he trained under the great master, Yip Man. In 1959, his parents sent him back to the US to university, where he studied drama at the University of Washington. He also began to teach martial arts and in 1964, he dropped out of college to teach full time.

Lee developed his own approach, abandoning the rigid and formal drills of traditional systems in favor of flexibility, speed and efficiency, as well as encouraging weight training and running to build strength and stamina. He called his system Jeet Kune Do, or 'the Way of the Intercepting Fist.' Working with leading US martial arts enthusiasts, such as the karate expert Ed Parker and the taekwondo master Jhoon Rhee, Lee made guest appearances at popular martial arts events, notably the Long Beach International Karate Championships and opened two martial arts schools.

As his profile rose, Lee was invited to audition for the TV series *The Green Hornet,* in which he appeared as Kato, the sidekick and bodyguard. He received more fan mail than the show's star and his performance inspired thousands to take up martial arts. Lee capitalized on this success, by providing personalized martial arts training for stars, such as Steve McQueen and James Coburn and his invaluable Hollywood connections led to guest appearances in a couple of films. He quickly became disillusioned, however, as it became clear that Hollywood was unlikely to cast him in a leading role and he returned to Hong Kong in 1971.

Soon after his return, he was snapped up by film director Raymond Chow to star in two movies. It was Lee's third film, *Way of the Dragon* (1972), with its legendary fight scenes with Chuck Norris, that ensured Lee's immortality as the world's most influential martial arts star. Hollywood finally accorded him the respect he sought in 1973, when he was cast as the star in *Enter the Dragon,* which catapulted him to global stardom. Despite his exceptional levels of fitness, Lee died suddenly, shortly before the film was released, which only accentuated his status as a cultural icon.

Left: Bruce Lee, in a scene from his iconic movie, *Enter the Dragon.*

Vivien Leigh

Born Vivian Mary Hartley
November 5, 1913
Darjeeling, India

Died July 7, 1967
London, England

Vivien Leigh was a classically beautiful English actress, best known for her marriage to Laurence Olivier and her electrifying performances in two of Hollywood's legendary movies, *Gone with the Wind* (1939) and *A Streetcar Named Desire* (1951).

Leigh's delicate beauty and classic English rose looks hid a fragile personality, blighted by bipolar disorder, which gave her a reputation as a 'difficult' star. Born in Darjeeling, India, where her father was an officer in the Indian cavalry, Leigh was educated in Europe, before enrolling at RADA (the Royal Academy of Dramatic Art) in London to train as an actress.

Aged only 19, Leigh was married, in 1932, to Herbert Leigh Holman, a barrister 13 years her senior, and gave up her dramatic ambitions to devote herself to her husband. However, she found domesticity restrictive and got a small part in an English film, *Things are Looking Up*, in 1935. Rejecting her agent's suggestion of the name April Morn, Vivian took the stage name Vivien Leigh, just altering the spelling of her first name. Having received good reviews for her role in the comedy *The Mask of Virtue* in London's West End, Leigh was spotted by Laurence Olivier. Their friendship developed into a full-blown affair on the set of *Fire Over England* (1937), their first movie together.

The professional pairing of Leigh and Olivier was a powerful one, with Leigh undoubtedly benefiting from Olivier's depth of understanding and great dramatic experience. They appeared together on the London stage, where Leigh was a frequent performer, before Olivier left for Hollywood in 1938. Leigh followed him, partly because she harbored tenacious ambitions to be cast as Scarlett O'Hara in the forthcoming *Gone with the Wind*. She was a surprising choice for the role, being relatively inexperienced, as well as English, but she gave the performance of her life as Scarlett. She won the Oscar for Best Actress, married Olivier in 1940 and became one half of the most celebrated couple in Hollywood.

She worked with Olivier in a number of films and plays throughout the 1940s, but struggled with both mental and physical health problems. Casting Leigh in the 1949 London stage production of *A Streetcar Named Desire* was contentious, because of the disturbing nature of the play. But her exhilarating performance allowed her to repeat the role in the film adaptation, opposite Marlon Brando in 1951, which won her a second Oscar.

In later years, Leigh said her role as Blanche DuBois 'tipped me over into madness' and the episodes of depression certainly became more frequent during the 1950s.

Divorced from Olivier in 1960, Leigh continued to work occasionally in the theatre and in film and died of tuberculosis in 1967, at the age of 53.

Below: Leigh played Blanche Dubois to great acclaim in the stage production of *A Streetcar Named Desire* in London in 1949.

Right: Leigh in her most famous role, as the spoilt southern belle, Scarlett O'Hara, in *Gone with the Wind*.

George Lucas

Born May 14, 1944
Modesto, California

The man who introduced Luke Skywalker and Indiana Jones to the world, George Lucas has made an immeasurable impact on the world of popular culture. He is one of the most successful and revered film-makers of modern times and has chosen his projects with great care, having directed only six major films. However, his credits as writer or producer are extensive and he has established a number of special effects companies to bring his innovative movie visions to the big screen.

Lucas was born in California and, as a teenager, he was obsessed with two things: film making and car racing. He attended the University of Southern California, School of Cinematic Art and became highly skilled in the technical aspects of cinematography.

Lucas's first movie, *THX 1138*, was an adaptation of a student project, and although it was a commercial failure, it is now a cult classic. Released in 1971 with support from Francis Ford Coppola, it was a science-fiction movie that explores a dystopian future and earned Lucas a reputation as an intelligent director of science fiction.

Lucas's second movie was a reaction to the commercial failure of *THX 1138*. *American Graffiti* (1973) was a nostalgic, semi-autobiographical film that wove together images of growing up in early 1960s America with a rock n' roll soundtrack. It was an instant hit and became one of the most profitable movies of the 1970s, partly because it had been made on a risible budget of just $775,000.

The profits from *American Graffiti* enabled Lucas to work independently on a project that had been rejected by Universal Studios, a movie called *Star Wars*. With a deceptively simple plot based around the struggle between good and evil, a long time ago in a galaxy far, far away, *Star Wars* (released in 1977) has become one of the most successful films of all time and spawned five further movies. The secret of Lucas' success is down to his incredible ingenuity and his uncompromising high standards in special effects. Quite simply, he captured the imagination of millions of fans. Uniquely in the history of cinema, he was able to revisit the franchise to release three 'prequel' movies, some 22 years after the original first appeared.

In the meantime, Lucas acted as writer, or producer on a series of box-office hits, often in conjunction with Steven Spielberg, most notably the Indiana Jones series that began in 1981 with *Raiders of the Lost Ark*. As with the *Star Wars* films the Indiana Jones series was inspired by the movie serials, such as *Flash Gordon*, that Lucas saw as a child. The films were so successful that Lucas revisited the franchise in 2008 when he released *Indiana Jones and the Kingdom of the Crystal Skull*.

Lucasfilm Ltd was formed in 1971 as Lucas' production company and its subsidiary, the Industrial Light & Magic Company, was founded in 1975 to create cutting-edge special effects. The company has won 14 Academy Awards for its work.

George Lucas has been involved in some of the most exciting and popular movies of all time, and is rightly held in high regard by fans and fellow film-makers alike.

Left: Lucas at the 30th anniversary screening of *Star Wars*, 2007.

Below: Lucas (left) with Harrison Ford (center) and Steven Spielberg (right) at a screening of *Indiana Jones and the Kingdom of the Crystal Skull* in Cannes, France, 2008.

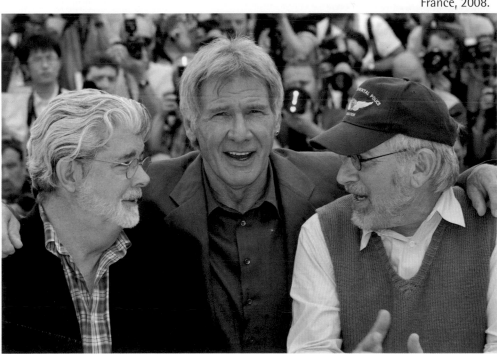

Baz Luhrmann

Born Mark Anthony Luhrmann
September 17, 1962
Sydney, New South
Wales, Australia

Imaginative and innovative, the movie director Baz Luhrmann is responsible for some of the best Australian films of recent years.

The roots of Luhrmann's success lie in his upbringing in a small town in the New South Wales countryside. His father was a Vietnam veteran, who insisted on crew cuts for his sons and a busy routine of creative activities. His parents' hobbies included ballroom dancing, and Baz has said of his home town, Heron's Creek, 'The town consisted of a gas station, a pig farm, a dress shop and a movie theatre – and we ran them all'. Baz loved storytelling and working at the gas station and in the cinema meant that he could meet and observe all kinds of people.

Luhrmann moved to Sydney when he was a teenager. His crew cut grew out (and his hair earned him the nickname 'Baz',

after Basil Brush, the BBC puppet) and he attended the prestigious National Institute of Dramatic Art, where, in 1986, he wrote and directed an award-winning 30-minute play called *Strictly Ballroom*, which in 1992, became his first movie. In the meantime, Luhrmann was drawn to theater and opera, and became well known for his inventive and imaginative productions.

In 1990 Luhrmann's lavish production of Puccini's *La Bohème* won the Mo Award for Operatic Performance of the Year and he followed this success with a Hindu version of Benjamin Britten's opera, *A Midsummer Night's Dream*, set in colonial India.

When his first movie, the romantic comedy *Strictly Ballroom*, was premiered at the 1992 Cannes Film Festival, it won the Prix de la Jeunesse. Critics and audiences praised the movie's appealing and unlikely combination of gritty

Australian humor and the torrid world of ballroom dancing contests.

This success earned Luhrmann a three-year contract with 20th Century Fox, and allowed him to produce his exhilarating modern interpretation of Shakespeare's *Romeo and Juliet* (1996). The movie, starring Leonardo di Caprio, retains the original Shakespearean dialogue, but appeals to modern audiences with its rock soundtrack and setting in modern America. It was instantly successful both commercially and critically.

Luhrmann's next movie, *Moulin Rouge* (2001), completed what has come to be called his 'Red Curtain Trilogy'. An elaborate musical set in 19th-century Paris, *Moulin Rouge* was immensely popular with audiences and was nominated for eight Academy Awards. Luhrmann next turned his considerable imagination to epic movies, releasing the ambitious historical romance *Australia* in 2008.

Luhrmann is regarded as one of the most instinctive and ingenious filmmakers at work today. His first three films are very different in terms of subject matter, but share simple storylines, a certain heightened reality and a creative device such as dance, poetry or music, to drive the action.

Left: Baz Luhrmann (center) takes a curtain call for his production of *La Bohème*, 2002.

Right: Arguably Australia's greatest film director, Luhrmann attends the premiere of *Australia*, 2008.

Madonna

Born Madonna Louise
Veronica Ciccone
August 16, 1958
Bay City, Michigan, USA

Singer Madonna's ever-changing image has made for one of the most interesting careers in rock history.

The best-selling female rock artist of the 20th century, she has never shied away from controversy, often exploiting it simply to promote her work. The popularity of her music, her ability to embrace and often start new trends, as well as her astute business sense, have given her a degree of influence in the music industry unusual for any female artist.

Originally intending to become a dancer, Madonna turned to music and signed with Sire records in 1982, releasing her debut single *Everybody* the same year. Her first album, *Madonna*, appeared in 1983 and produced a couple of chart singles. But it was her smash hit 1984 album, *Like a Virgin*, that established her image and shot the 'Material Girl' on to the world stage. Her next album, *True Blue* (1986), was a bestseller in 25 countries, producing three singles including the controversial *Papa Don't Preach*. The first female artist fully to exploit the power of music videos, she used them to give her songs an added visual punch as she explored religious symbolism and sexual themes in her work. *Like a Prayer*, released in 1989, received widespread critical acclaim and predictably, in view of the images of burning crosses in the video, condemnation from the Vatican.

The spectacular 'Blonde Ambition' tour of 1990 was a visual feast of provocative choreography and superlative music that delighted fans. Keen to have complete creative control over her work, Madonna founded her own entertainment company, Maverick, in 1992 and published her first book of photography, starkly entitled *Sex*, which was preceded by the album *Erotica*.

Perhaps surprised that her deliberately edgy work did not attract more favorable reviews, she appeared to mellow in the mid-1990s, as she paused to have her first child, daughter Lourdes.

Madonna has periodically branched out into film, appearing in some 20 movies, with mixed results. One of her earliest, *Desperately Seeking Susan* (1985), was a hit, but the following year *Shanghai Surprise* (with first husband Sean Penn) flopped. Probably her most successful role was as Eva Perón in the musical *Evita*, which won her a Golden Globe award in 1996. Her concerts and tours, however, have broken box office records, with her 2008 'Sticky and Sweet' tour grossing $280 million – more than any other tour by a solo artist.

Madonna divorced her second husband, Guy Ritchie and then apparently took up with a man 28 years her junior, called Jesus. But after nearly 30 years in the business, the 'Queen of Pop' retains her capacity to thrill and surprise her fans. Feisty, opinionated and hugely talented, Madonna continues to turn out the fantastic pop records that have made her the most successful female recording artist of all time.

Left: Always an exciting live performer, Madonna plays in Rome, 2008, during her 'Sticky and Sweet' tour.

Right: 'Blonde Ambition' – Madonna's provocative 1990 tour, which was slated by the Catholic church, but highly praised by musical critics.

Nelson Mandela

Born Rolihlahla Mandela
July 18, 1918
Mvezo, South Africa

Nelson Mandela is one of the most highly respected elder statesman in the world. In 1990 he emerged from his 27 years of imprisonment at the hands of South Africa's Apartheid regime with a dignity and forbearance strong enough to unite his troubled country and heal the wounds caused by racial strife. He became the first black President of South Africa in 1994.

The story of Mandela's long life is inspirational. Born the son of a tribal chief, Mandela trained as a lawyer and in 1942 joined the African National Congress Party (ANC), which fought to end the Apartheid laws in South Africa. After the victory of the hardline Afrikaaner Party in the 1948 elections, Mandela began to take an active part in politics, inspired by Gandhi in India, he advocated non-violent civil disobedience to the government's laws of segregation. In 1952 the ANC launched the Campaign for Defiance of Unjust Laws, and Mandela's part in organizing resistance earned him a suspended prison sentence. In fact, Mandela spent most of the 1950s on the edge of the law – despite his attempts to practice as an attorney. He was banned, arrested, and imprisoned, and was one of the 156 people accused in the Treason Trial of 1956–61. After the Sharpeville Massacre in 1960 the ANC was outlawed and Mandela helped to form the armed wing of the ANC in preparation for an armed struggle.

This was not a decision he took lightly, but Mandela and his colleagues could see no other way. He later wrote: 'It was only when all else had failed, when all channels of peaceful protest had been barred to us, that the decision was made

to embark on violent forms of political struggle.' Inevitably, as the leader of the armed wing Umkhonto we Sizwe and after 17 months on the run, Mandela was arrested in 1962 and sentenced to five years in prison. Two years later he was tried in the Rivonia Trial, on charges of sabotage and planning armed action, as well as conspiracy to help a foreign power to invade. Together with Walter Sisulu and Govan Mbeki, Mandela was found guilty and the three were sentenced to life imprisonment.

A generation later, with the Apartheid regime condemned around the world, Mandela was finally released from his prison on Robben Island in 1990. He became leader of the ANC and worked with F. W. de Klerk, the South African President, to effect a peaceful transfer of power to a non-racial democracy within South Africa. The work of the two men

was recognized in the joint award of the 1993 Nobel Peace Prize and in 1994, in the country's first multiracial elections, Mandela was elected President of South Africa.

Mandela retired from politics in 1999, renowned as a charismatic man of great moral integrity.

Left: Nelson Mandela at the 2007 ceremony to restore the Mandela clan chieftaincy, in Mandela's natal village of Mvezo. Mandela's grandson Mandla was made a chief, some 87 years after a white magistrate removed the title.

Below: Nelson and Winnie Mandela on their wedding day, 1958.

Overleaf: Mandela with President F.W. de Klerk in 1994, shortly after they won the Nobel Peace Prize.

Marcel Marceau

Born Marcel Mangel
March 22, 1923
Strasbourg, France

Died Died September 27, 2007
Cahors, France

Marceau's extraordinary career as the most famous mime artist in the world began not in the circus, or on the stage, but while working as a member of the French Resistance during World War II.

Born in Strasbourg, France, the son of a Jewish butcher, Marcel Mangel and his family changed their name to Marceau to escape the attention of the occupying German authorities during the second World War. Marcel and his brother joined the Resistance and it was to keep young Jewish children quiet, while they were escaping from the Nazis, that he used his miming skills. After the liberation of Paris in 1944, Marceau worked as a liaison officer for the French army, working with the American forces.

Shortly after he was demobilized, he enrolled at Charles Dullin's School of Dramatic Art in Paris and studied under the great mime master, Etienne Decroux. While still a student, he was inspired by the work of his great hero, Charlie Chaplin, to invent the character of Bip the Clown, a perennially doleful, white-faced clown, clad in a striped sweater, with a battered silk opera hat. Named for Pip in Dickens' *Great Expectations*, Bip epitomized the innocent alone in a world that was both terrifying and amazing and like Chaplin's Little Tramp, he was both downtrodden and rebellious.

Bip was to remain Marceau's most famous creation. Perhaps as a result of his wartime experiences, Marceau was a great believer in the strength of the human spirit. ' We know that the fighting spirit of man is everlasting,' he explained: 'Death is absurd, but humanity has to be eternal.' Marceau appeared as Bip on stage and on screen around the world for over 50 years, but it was his theatrical work that was most successful, as he performed most strongly in front of live audiences.

He established the Compagnie de Mime Marcel Marceau in 1949 and first toured the US in 1955. In New York, his show had to be moved from the Phoenix Theatre to the Barrymore, a much larger venue, to accommodate the huge audiences. Aiming to spread 'L'art du silence' (the art of silence), Marceau became immensely popular in the US, where he made many television appearances. He undertook 40 world tours, the last one in 2006, shortly before he died. Marceau was showered with honors, notably the Légion d'honneur in France and was also widely known for his humanitarian work with the United Nations.

A delightful and charming interviewee, Marceau told journalists, 'Never get a mime talking. He won't stop.' But his ability to convey complex tales and emotions in silent gestures elevated mime to a highly regarded art form and influenced a new generation of entertainers. Michael Jackson's 'moonwalk' was probably inspired by Marceau and Rowan Atkinson's Mr Bean character undoubtedly owes a debt to him.

Left and far left: Marceau drew his inspiration from the classical Pierrot clowns, as well as Charlie Chaplin's character, the Little Tramp. He performed all over the world to spread what he called 'the art of silence.'

Bob Marley

Born Robert Nesta Marley
February 6, 1945
St. Ann, Jamaica

Died May 11, 1981
Miami, Florida, USA

Bob Marley was the foremost reggae artist of his generation, a pioneering musician, who transported reggae from the Caribbean to the wider world stage.

Born in the rural parish of St. Ann, Jamaica, Marley was the son of Norval Marley, a Jamaican Royal Marine officer of English descent and Cedella Booker, a young Afro-Jamaican. He left school at 14 and took himself off to Kingston to make music, meeting Neville 'Bunny' Livingston (later better known as Bunny Wailer) and Peter Tosh. Together they founded the Wailers, along with Junior Braithwaite, Cherry Smith and Beverley Kelso, in 1963. In 1964, their first single, *Simmer Down*, was a huge hit in Jamaica and they recorded some 20 singles, but with the departure of Braithwaite and Kelso in 1965 and a lack of income, in 1966, the Wailers disbanded. Marley stayed with his mother in Newark, Delaware, working in a factory, before returning to Jamaica in 1967, where he became a devout Rastafarian.

The Wailers reunited and under the guidance of Lee 'Scratch' Perry, from 1969 recorded popular local hits, but the Jamaican record industry simply did not have the money, or influence to launch acts on to the international scene. The Wailers finally got a break when Chris Blackwell signed them to Island Records and with the release of their first album, *Catch a Fire*, in 1973, they got the international recognition they so richly deserved. *Burnin'*, issued in 1974, included the hit *I Shot the Sheriff*, which was covered by Eric Clapton, raising Marley's profile still further. Having made an overseas tour in 1973, the Wailers disbanded in 1974, with Tosh and Livingston embarking on solo careers.

With a changed line-up that now included his wife, Rita, Marley continued to perform with the Wailers and toured Europe, Africa and the Americas. The outstanding track on their next album, *Natty Dread* (1974), was the soul-reggae ballad *No Woman, No Cry*, probably Marley's most popular song and his first Top 40 hit in the UK. With a particularly

loyal fan base in Britain, the Wailers had further hits with *Exodus* (1977), *Jamming* (1977) and *Is This Love* (1978).

Following a regular pattern of an album a year, followed by a concert tour, Marley established himself as an international star at the end of the 1970s, but his heart and his roots remained in Jamaica. He took new inspiration from Africa, after touring Gabon in 1978, which was reflected in his 1979 album *Survival*. Such was his status, that he was invited to perform at Zimbabwe's independence celebrations in 1980.

Just as he had succeeded in establishing reggae as more than just a minority music, Marley died from cancer at the tragically early age of 36. Revered, loved and admired, he was given a state funeral in Jamaica.

Left: Marley, with his characteristic dreadlocks, performing in 1978.

Below: Marley (center) flanked by Bunny Wailer (left) and Peter Tosh (right), in 1964, the year of their first hit.

Ann Miller

Born Johnnie Lucille
Ann Collier
April 12, 1923
Chirno, Texas, USA
Died
January 22, 2004
Los Angeles, California,
USA

In her heyday, in the musicals of the 1940s and 1950s, Ann Miller was a dancing sensation, able to perform an incredible 500 dance taps a minute. She appeared in a number of films, generally as the second female lead. She never attained the starry status of other legends, such as Ginger Rogers, but her flamboyantly glamorous appearance made her a screen legend.

Miler's father wanted a boy, so, rather unusually, she was christened Johnnie, but she was often known as Annie. Her mother took her to dancing classes to help her recover from the rickets that afflicted her as a small child and she displayed a prodigious talent from an early age. When her parents split up, she and her mother moved to California,

where Ann began dancing in cabaret clubs, apparently as young as 13. She was discovered by the actress Lucille Ball in 1937 and she was given a contract with RKO. She claimed to be 18 – in fact she was only 14 years old.

Her first non-speaking role was in *New Faces of 1937* and she followed this with a few light romantic comedies, usually playing a dancer or young innocent in movies, such as *Stage Door* (1938) and *Too Many Girl*s (1940). In the early 1940s she became popular in pre-war morale-boosting films such as *Priorities on Parade* (1942) and *Reveille with Beverley* (1943). Miller somehow never made the leap to the leading female role, even though she aspired to the kind of romantic parts offered to other dancing

stars like Ginger Rogers. Many years later she said, 'At MGM, I always played the second feminine lead; I was never the star in films, I was the brassy, good-hearted showgirl. I never really had my big moment on the screen.'

However, she was excellent in the roles she had and really hit her stride in the great musical movies of the late 1940s and early 1950s. Her finest hour was *Easter Parade* (1948), a role she only won because the first choice, Cyd Charisse, broke her leg. She had to dance in flat shoes so that she didn't appear taller than Fred Astaire.

With the decline of the musicals, Miller's career altered at the end of the 1950s, as she moved to work in nightclubs and on TV programs such as *The Ed Sullivan Show*. She appeared on Broadway in 1969 in *Mame*, a role that was immensely popular and won critical praise. She became well known for her glamor, especially her big, bouffant, black hairstyles and heavily kohled eyes. She made her last movie appearance in David Lynch's *Mulholland Drive* (2001). Although she never had her 'big moment', Ann Miller was a legendary dancer. In a final tribute, her tap shoes are housed in the Smithsonian Museum, Washington DC.

Left: Ann Miller shows off her dancing talent in the revival of *Sugar Babes* on Broadway, 1979.

Right: A 1948 Hollywood publicity still of a glamorous young Ann Miller.

Mickey Mouse

Created November 18, 1928
Los Angeles, California, USA

Mickey Mouse was the first and arguably the greatest international cartoon character created during the 20th century. Instantly recognizable, with his round black ears, red shorts and pert snout, Mickey was the creation of Walt Disney, the animation genius known as 'the man behind the mouse.'

Since his creation in 1928, Mickey has become an icon, not only of the Disney Company, but also of the USA – a cultural symbol of America recognized around the world. Inspired by the pet he kept as a child, Disney dreamed up the idea of a cute mouse character, who was originally christened Mortimer Mouse. Drawn by Disney's long-time collaborator Ub Iwerks, Mickey (renamed by Disney's wife, Lillian) featured in two poorly received short animations, before appearing in his first talkie, *Steamboat Willie*, in November 1928. With sound movies only a year old, audiences were thrilled to hear sound used in an animated cartoon feature and Mickey was voiced by Disney himself, who had succeeded in taking advantage of the popular new technology.

Iwerks and Disney parted company in 1930, but Mickey lived on, as other animators were recruited to draw him. During the lean Depression years, Mickey became immensely popular, starring in a string of short animated features, in a variety of anthropomorphic roles, but rarely as an actual mouse. Initially black and white, Mickey did not appear in color until 1935.

In 1930, the Mickey Mouse comic strip was syndicated to newspapers across the USA, with the first strips drawn by Ub Iwerks. After he had left and another artist had quickly moved on, Walt Disney asked a third artist, Floyd Gottfredson, to take over temporarily. He continued to draw the strip for the next 45 years until he retired in 1975.

Mickey starred in over 120 different animated cartoons, alongside a family of characters – Minnie, Goofy, Pluto, Donald Duck and others. His success lay in his versatility – he could appear as anything, in any walk of life. Mischievous, courageous, romantic, misguided and often heroic, he was Everymouse and audiences loved him.

In 1932, Disney was awarded a special Academy Award for his creation, an honor that recognized the skill of his team of animators. On screen, Mickey has not aged, but he has been subtly altered over the years, notably, in *The Pointer* (1939), where animator, Fred Moore, gave Mickey's eyes pupils, to make them more expressive.

In the 1950s, Disney grasped the new challenges of television and from 1955 Mickey hosted *The Mickey Mouse Club*, which became the most successful children's show on television. Revived in the 1970s, the program was succeeded in 1999 by computer-animated educational shows for the Disney Channel – *Mickey Mouse Works*, Disney's *House of Mouse* and more recently, *Mickey Mouse Clubhouse*.

The amazing longevity of Disney's most popular creation is due to the universal charm of Mickey's character. Funny, cute, plucky, innocent and optimistic, he has appealed to the better side of human nature across the generations.

Right and below: Created in 1928, Mickey was quickly joined by a host of cartoon friends. Minnie first appeared in the short animation *Plane Crazy* in 1928 and the following year, in *Mickey's Follies*, it became clear that she was Mickey's girlfriend.

Kylie Minogue

Singer and actress, Kylie is one of a handful of entertainers universally known by her first name. Officially the most played female artist on UK radio, for two decades she has successfully marketed her own brand of immensely catchy pop.

Born in Melbourne, Kylie was a child actor in Australia, joining the cast of the soap opera *Neighbours* in 1986, as Charlene Robinson and playing opposite Jason Donovan. Their partnership was a crucial part of the show's success, in both Australia and Britain. Their screen wedding, in 1987, was watched by 20 million viewers in the UK, where Kylie's girl-next-door appeal won her millions of fans.

With her petite frame, outsized by her gutsy voice and showgirl charisma, Kylie seamlessly made the transition from soap superstar to global singing sensation in the late 1980s. In 1987, she became a part of the Stock, Aitken and Waterman hit-making machine, after releasing a cover version of the 1962 song *The Loco-Motion*, which became Australia's best-selling single of the 1980s. She recorded *I Should be So Lucky* that same year. An instant pop hit, the song reached No. 1 in the UK and Australia, while Kylie returned home to work on *Neighbours*. Her singing career began to outshine her acting after the release of her first album, *Kylie*, in 1988, which generated five Top Ten singles in Australia, the UK and parts of Europe.

Kylie's dance-pop music was popular, chart-topping and lucrative, but it was regarded rather snootily by music critics. In 1990, Kylie broke away from Stock, Aitken and Waterman to promote herself as a more mature, sexy artist, directing her own music videos and launching a new phase in her career. Influenced by musicians, such as Nick Cave and Michael Hutchence of INXS, Kylie became more creative. Her collaboration album, *Impossible Princess* (1997), became her most successful release since *Kylie* in 1988.

In the 1990s, Kylie appeared to be guided by more experienced members of the music business, but by the early 2000s no one could be in any doubt that she was in charge of her own career.

She acknowledged a (small) debt to Madonna in one interview: 'We both like to keep an eye on what's happening – trends. She's definitely the front-runner in this business, but I share her enthusiasm for being experimental ... And I've got a good commercial head on my shoulders.' In the early years of the new century, Kylie's stage acts became more extravagant, inspired by burlesque performances and Broadway musicals. The 'Showgirl' tour was interrupted by her successful treatment for breast cancer in 2005–6.

Kylie has shrewdly managed her image throughout her career and confounded critics with record sales and airplay that are the true testimony to her popularity around the world.

Born	Kylie Ann Minogue May 28, 1968 Melbourne, Victoria, Australia

Left: Britain is home to some of Kylie's most devoted fans. Here she performs in Hyde Park, London, 2009.

Below: Kylie Minogue on stage at Le Bataclan in Paris, 2001.

Born Norma Jeane Mortenson
June 1, 1926
Los Angeles, California,
USA

Died August 5, 1962
Los Angeles, California,
USA

The ultimate blonde bombshell, Hollywood glamour girl and confused victim, actress and singer Marilyn Monroe, had an appeal that glows as vividly today as it did in her short lifetime.

Born to an unstable mother and an unnamed runaway father, Marilyn spent much of her childhood in foster homes and orphanages, marrying for the first time at 16. She was talent-spotted by a photographer in 1944 and began her lifelong love affair with the camera as a model.

After two years, she signed her first studio contract with 20th Century Fox, dyed her hair blonde and changed her name. Her early film roles were unremarkable (as indeed were many of her later ones). She first attracted serious attention in 1950, in two minor and already typecast roles, first in John Huston's thriller *The Asphalt Jungle* as the gangster's luscious moll and then, in *All About Eve*, as a dim blonde among urban sophisticates. Fox recognized her screen potential and put her into a series of films in the early 1950s. *Tense Niagara,* the delightfully funny *Gentlemen Prefer Blondes* and *How to Marry a Millionaire* – all made in 1953 – together lifted her to superstardom. Her brief marriage to baseball star, Joe DiMaggio, dates from this time.

In 1955, determined to take control of her career and to master the stage fright that contributed to a reputation for unreliability, Monroe took a break from filming to study acting with Lee Strasberg in New York and *Bus Stop* (1956) proved that she could turn in a straight dramatic performance. The press had fun with her relationship at this time with famous playwright Arthur Miller, calling the pair 'the Egghead and the Hourglass'. They married in 1956 and for a time were ecstatically happy; Miller described her as 'a whirling light ... all paradox and mystery'. *Some Like It Hot* (1959) was a huge success, gaining Monroe a Golden Globe award, although it relegated her to 'dumb blonde' status again. Miller wrote the screenplay of *The Misfits* (1960) as a gift for her, but by the time the film was shot, their marriage had fallen apart and Marilyn turned in a dispiriting performance.

If her screen roles are of variable quality, her musical numbers are enchanting – from *Diamonds are a Girl's Best Friend* in *Gentlemen Prefer Blondes* and *I Want to Be Loved by You* in *Some Like It Hot*, to *My Heart Belongs to Daddy* in Cukor's *Let's Make Love* (1960). It was her singing of 'Happy Birthday' at a party for President Kennedy in May 1962, that opened the last mysterious phase of her life, with allegations of affairs with both Jack and Bobby Kennedy. Popular doubt persists as to the real cause of her death, reportedly from a drug overdose, but her luminous beauty, feminine sensuality and allure, combined with a childlike vulnerability, have ensured her iconic status.

Right: Iconic and fabulous - Marilyn at her most glamorous, 1953.

Below: With John Huston (left) and husband Arthur Miller (right) on the set of her last movie, *The Misfits*.

Overleaf: Marilyn Monroe and Tom Ewell in an iconic scene from the 1955 movie *The Seven Year Itch*.

Jim Morrison

Born James Douglas Morrison
December 8, 1943
Melbourne, Florida, USA

Died July 3, 1971
Paris, France

Singer, songwriter, poet and Sixties wild child, Jim Morrison was the prototype of the gifted and troubled rock star. As lead singer and lyricist of the psychedelic rock band, The Doors, his charismatic, scandalous and unpredictable performances made rock history.

Morrison had an itinerant childhood, as his father was a career US Navy officer, but by 1964, he had moved to the West Coast of America and was studying film at UCLA. After graduating, he led a bohemian intellectual life, hanging out with writers and journalists in Venice Beach, reading Nietzsche, Rimbaud and Kerouac and writing poetry. In 1965, he formed The Doors with former fellow student and keyboardist, Ray Manzarek and they were soon joined by drummer, John Densmore and guitarist, Robby Krieger. They took the band's name from the title of a book by Aldous Huxley, about his experiences with the drug mescaline, *The Doors of Perception*, which in turn was a quote from visionary poet, William Blake. Both the poetic and the drug links were to prove fundamental for Morrison.

In June 1966, The Doors played the prestigious Whisky a Go Go club on Sunset Boulevard, as support group for Van Morrison's band, Them. Jim's developing stage persona, with its recklessness and air of menace, was influenced by Van Morrison. The band signed to Elektra in 1966 and their first album, *The Doors*, included their first hit single *Light My Fire*, which made the No. 1 slot on the Billboard singles chart and sold over a million copies. The song was largely written by Krieger – the band collaborated on many of their lyrics – but it was Morrison's baritone voice and the dark-edged eroticism of his performance that caught public attention. The famous 'Young Lion' photo session in 1967 immortalized Morrison in his rock icon role.

The Doors' next album, *Strange Days* (1967), featured more of Morrison's elliptical, wide-ranging, pseudo-poetic lyrics, including the title track, which reflected on the emerging hippy youth culture and *People are Strange*, about alienation. His own alienation was growing stronger and more troublesome. He would turn up late for live performances or drunk for recordings and the band took a lengthy break in 1969, before recording the last album that Morrison made, *LA Woman*.

Meanwhile Morrison had self-published two volumes of poetry and recorded some of his poems in a professional sound studio. In a performance in Louisiana, to publicize *LA Woman*, Morrison appeared to have a breakdown on stage, refusing to perform for the rest of the gig and his fellow musicians decided to cut short the live act.

Morrison moved to Paris, apparently intending to become a writer in exile, like so many of his heroes, but within three months he was dead, probably from a heroin overdose.

Left: Wild and charismatic, Morrison thrilled fans.

Below: The Doors in LA, 1969. They were one of the most controversial rock acts of the 1960s, partly because of Morrison's unpredictable behavior.

Paul Newman

Born Paul Leonard Newman
January 26, 1925
Cleveland, Ohio, USA

Died September 26, 2008
Westport, Connecticut,
USA

The ultimate all-American blue-eyed boy, Paul Newman was the great Hollywood survivor, whose charisma and talent secured him substantial roles, throughout a film career spanning over 50 years.

A much acclaimed actor, with one Oscar for Scorsese's *The Color of Money* (1986) and eight nominations, he was also a film director, philanthropist, entrepreneur, car-race enthusiast and unusually for Hollywood, devoted family man.

Born to parents who ran a sporting goods store, Newman showed an early interest in the theater. After naval service, in the Pacific during World War II, he studied drama at Yale and with Lee Strasberg in New York, making his Broadway debut in 1953.

The first Hollywood role followed almost immediately and in 1955, he landed the part of boxer, Rocky Graziano, in *Somebody Up There Likes Me.* The part, originally intended for James Dean, established his film persona as the tough kid who makes good. In 1957, a landmark year, he won a Golden Globe for Most Promising Newcomer and began his lifelong relationship with actor Joanne Woodward – they met on the set of *The Long Hot Summer* and married a year later. *Cat on a Hot Tin Roof* with Elizabeth Taylor (1958), based on the play by Tennessee Williams, gave him the chance to turn in a more subtle performance, as the neurotic alcoholic, Brick and earned him his first Oscar nomination.

Newman was one of a minority of screen idols from the last days of the 1950s star system, who remained a box office draw in the grittier movies of the 1960s and 1970s. His rebellious screen persona, allied with his personal charm, led to a stream of good parts, beginning with perhaps his most memorable role of all, the cocky pool shark in the downbeat atmospheric drama *The Hustler* (1961). *Hud* (1964), *Cool Hand Luke* (1967) and *The Life and Times of Judge Roy Bean* (1972) all played to the tough-guy image, while his two classic films with Robert Redford, *Butch Cassidy and the Sundance Kid* (1969) and *The Sting* (1973), added charm and humor, to make an irresistible package.

Newman also directed several feature films, some of them starring his wife, Joanne Woodward, such as the Oscar-nominated *Rachel, Rachel* (1968) and *The Glass Menagerie* (1987). At the same time, Newman was indulging his taste for auto racing, winning at Thompson, Connecticut, in 1972 and coming second at Le Mans, France, in 1979. Meanwhile, the parts kept rolling in, with *The Towering Inferno* (1974), *The Verdict* (1982), *The Color of Money* – in which he reprised his hustler character – and his Oscar-nominated Irish mobster in *Road to Perdition* (2002). His food company, founded as a charitable concern in the 1980s, became a million dollar business. When his death (from lung cancer) was announced, every theater on Broadway dimmed its lights, in tribute to one of their own.

Left: Newman on the set of *Hud*, 1962, for which he won an Oscar nomination.

Right: *Fort Apache – the Bronx* was a huge success at the time of its release in 1981, largely due to Newman's performance.

Jack Nicholson

Charismatic film actor Jack Nicholson has an extraordinary Oscar record, with nominations in every decade since the 1960s.

In a sequence of landmark roles, in films from the brilliant *One Flew Over the Cuckoo's Nest* (1975), through *The Shining* (1980) and *The Witches of Eastwick* (1987), to *Batman* (1989), Nicholson has created a classic screen persona, as the droll, enigmatic, contradictory – and sometimes dangerous – non-conformist, reveling in the opportunity to cause havoc.

Nicholson was brought up to believe that his mother was his sister and his grandparents his parents. He soon moved to Los Angeles, where he started out in low-budget films in the 1950s. He finally made his mark – and won his first Oscar nomination – with a support role, as the hard-drinking lawyer in the road movie *Easy Rider* (1969), while his subtle and nuanced performance as the dogged private eye in Chinatown (1974) made him a star. *One Flew Over the Cuckoo's Nest* might well not have been made without Nicholson's status and support, together with his willingness to act in an ensemble. The result was well-deserved Oscars for star, film, script and director, but his wonderfully over-the-top characterization of the irrepressibly subversive McMurphy led to some limiting and typecast roles and a tendency to self-parody.

Born John Joseph Nicholson
April 22, 1937
New York City, or
Neptune, New Jersey, USA
(sources differ)

The 1980s, though, saw some more challenging parts. In Warren Beatty's epic *Reds* (1981), Nicholson turned in a controlled (and Oscar-nominated) performance, as the remote, but romantic playwright, Eugene O'Neill and his touchingly boisterous ex-astronaut who courts Shirley MacLaine in *Terms of Endearment* (1983), was an Oscar winner. After his wonderfully dim Mafia hitman in *Prizzi's Honor* (1985), playing opposite long-term girlfriend, Anjelica Huston, Nicholson returned to wildly funny outrageousness, as the sinister Daryl Van Horne in *The Witches of Eastwick*. The revelation that he was expecting a child with actress and model, Rebecca Broussard, ended the relationship with Huston.

The mix of serious acting and bombastic role play continued to characterize Nicholson's roles into the 1990s. Yet another Oscar nomination came for his commanding officer covering up a murder in *A Few Good Men* (1992). He neatly combined the serious and comedic in *Wolf* (1994), as a book editor, who turns into a werewolf, with a convincingly low-key performance.

More recent roles have been quieter, more reflective, even sadder and Nicholson has mostly chosen to work with old friends. His sharp performance as the curmudgeonly author, who falls for single mother Helen Hunt in *As Good as It Gets* (1997) won him a third Oscar, while his understated and sympathetic playing of a widowed salesman in *About Schmidt* (2002) earned him a 12th nomination, breaking his own record as the most nominated male actor in Oscar history.

Left: *The Shining* was one of Nicholson's most significant roles.

Right: 'I don't want people to know what I'm actually like. It's not good for an actor,' said enigmatic Nicholson, who played the Joker in *Batman*.

Barack Obama

Born Barack Hussein Obama
August 4, 1961
Honolulu, Hawaii, USA

American lawyer, author and politician, Barack Obama made history by becoming the first African-American president of the USA in January 2009.

Born in Honolulu, to a black African father from Kenya and a white American mother from Kansas, Obama moved, in 1967, with his mother to Indonesia, returning to Honolulu to live with his grandparents in 1971, for his schooling. He later wrote of the value of his experience in Hawaii, where a variety of cultures interacted in a climate of mutual respect. He went on to college in Los Angeles and then studied at Columbia University, New York, graduating in political science.

In 1985, Obama made a career-defining move to Chicago, to work in public service, as a community organizer on the tough South Side. Moving to Harvard Law School in 1988, he gained national attention (and the offer of a book contract, for the celebrated *Dreams From My Father*, published in 1995) by becoming the first black president of the *Harvard Law Review*. He continued to work in Chicago each summer, meeting his future wife, Michelle Robinson, at this time and returned there in 1991 to teach constitutional law at the University of Chicago and to join a small civil rights law firm.

Obama ran successfully for a seat in the Illinois Senate in 1996, where he championed social welfare reforms. He first ran (unsuccessfully) for Congress in

2000, but in 2004, stunned the Illinois Democrats with an emphatic win, against six challengers, in the state primary to select a Senate candidate. In July 2004, he seemed to have come from nowhere, when he delivered an electrifying keynote address at the Democratic National Convention. 'The Audacity of Hope' was instantly dubbed one of the best keynote speeches of the modern era. Suddenly, he was viewed as a possible leader, even a possible president and he won his Senate seat a few months later, with 70 per cent of the vote.

Obama's presidential campaign, beginning in February 2007, broke numerous records. In an eventual two-horse race, he beat Hillary Clinton to gain the Democratic presidential nomination in 2008. He clinched the presidential election with 53 per cent of the popular vote, against John McCain's 46 per cent, to become the USA's 44th president.

The first months of the Obama presidency were overshadowed by global economic crisis. In February 2009, a $787 billion economic stimulus package aided recovery, while GM and Chrysler, both huge employers, were bailed out. Clear indicators of a massive policy shift included the announcement of the closure of Guantanamo Bay detention center, a timetable for the withdrawal of US forces from Iraq, restrictions lifted on stem cell research and a proactive engagement with foreign policy issues, particularly the Middle East. The passing of a (much fought over) healthcare bill in January 2010 and the announcement of a nuclear limitation agreement with Russia in March, made for a productive first year in office.

Left and overleaf: Obama said, 'I stand here knowing that my story is part of the larger American story . . . and that in no other country on Earth is my story even possible.' His rise to power is the embodiment of the American dream.

Below: With his family on Inauguration Day, January 2009.

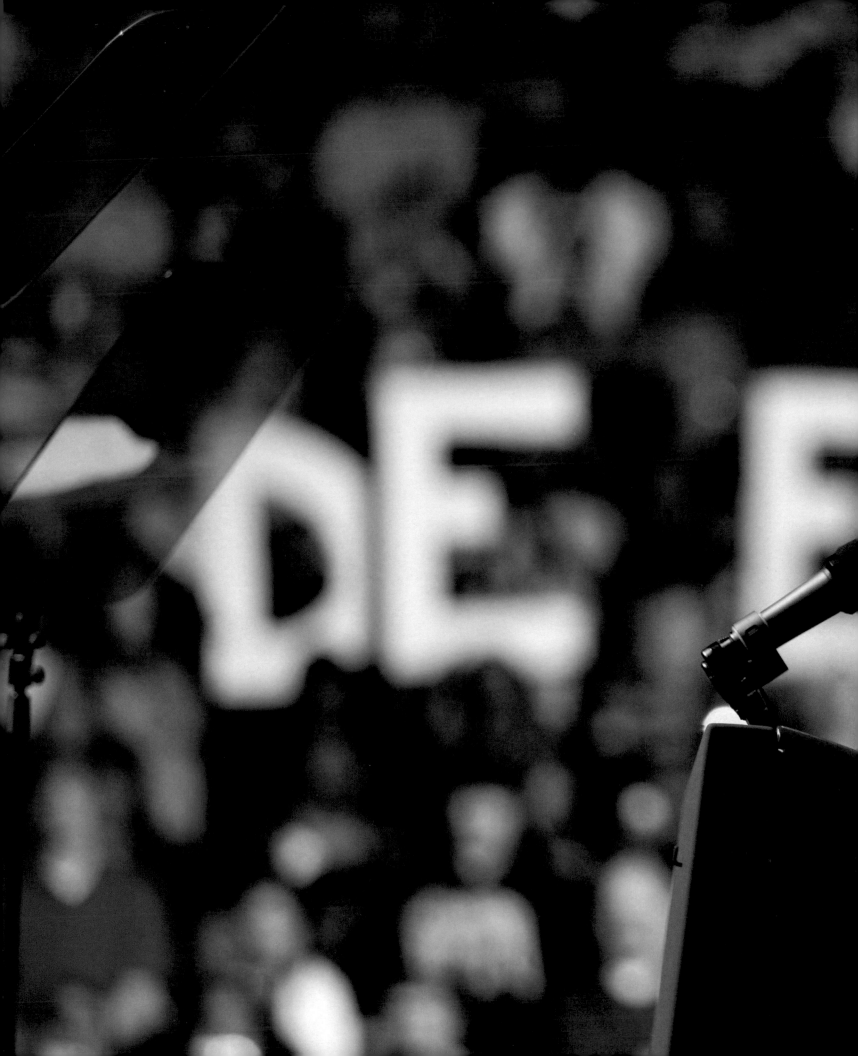

Laurence Olivier

Born Laurence Kerr Olivier
May 22, 1907
Dorking, Surrey, England

Died July 11, 1989
Steyning, West Sussex,
England

Acclaimed English actor, director and co-founder of the National Theatre in London, Laurence Olivier was one of the most revered actors of his generation on both stage and screen. In his long career he played everything from the heroic king in Shakespeare's *Henry V* (1944) to the terrifying villain with dentist's drill in *Marathon Man* (1976).

The young actor's stage breakthrough came in 1930, in the London production of Noël Coward's *Private Lives*. By 1931 he was in Hollywood, playing the romantic lead. Film was not his preferred medium, however and he was soon back on stage in England, alternating the roles of Romeo and Mercutio with his professional rival, John Gielgud, in Shakespeare's *Romeo and Juliet* (1935). This led to a series of star Shakespearean roles for impresario Lilian Baylis, at the Old Vic Theatre in London, where his roles included Henry V, Coriolanus, Iago and Hamlet, the latter opposite Vivien Leigh, as Ophelia.

When Olivier returned to Hollywood to play Heathcliff in *Wuthering Heights* (1939), Leigh soon followed to make her successful bid to play Scarlett O'Hara in *Gone With the Wind*. The success of both movies, with Olivier nominated for and Leigh winning an Oscar, made them both international celebrities. Olivier's next two films, both made in 1940, were classics – Hitchcock's *Rebecca* and *Pride and Prejudice*, with Greer Garson. Olivier and Vivien Leigh were married the same year.

World War II saw the couple back in England, with Olivier training as a pilot and serving two years in the Fleet Air Arm. In 1944, he was released from service to form a new Old Vic Theatre Company, performing a whole series of classic and modern plays to eager wartime and postwar audiences. He also directed his first film, *Henry V*, a glorious flight of fancy which starts within the confines of Shakespeare's Globe Theatre and takes wing into film. He went on to direct films of *Hamlet* (1948) and *Richard III* (1955).

Olivier's principal postwar commitment was to the long-planned National Theatre, of which he was co-founder and inaugural director. He opened in *Hamlet* (1963) and during the ten years of his directorship, acted in 12 plays and directed nine. Film-making at this time proved a welcome distraction and then became a necessity, when his marriage to Joan Plowright, in 1962, produced three children to support. He received Oscar nominations for his roles in the ingenious thriller *Sleuth* (1972), *Marathon Man* and *The Boys from Brazil* (1978).

Olivier was knighted in 1947. In 1970, he became the first actor to be created a life peer and in 1984, the Laurence Olivier Awards (for London theatre productions) were named in his honor. However, he always preferred to be addressed not as Sir Laurence, or Lord Olivier, but simply as Larry.

Left: Henry V, produced during World War II as a morale-boosting film, was one of Olivier's finest roles.

Below: Olivier won his tenth Oscar nomination for his role in The Boys from Brazil.

Jacqueline Kennedy Onassis

Born Jacqueline Lee Bouvier
July 28, 1929
Southampton, New York,
USA

Died May 19, 1994
New York, USA

First Lady, stunning beauty and fashion icon, Jackie Kennedy revitalized the White House during her husband's cruelly curtailed presidency and permanently changed the public perception of the First Lady's role.

Born into a comfortably wealthy and well-established New York family, Jackie had a traditional upbringing and made her society debut in 1947, when she was named Debutante of the Year. She was also smart and artistic, attending Vassar College and spending a student year in Grenoble, France. She married the then Senator, John F. 'Jack' Kennedy, in 1953, two years after graduating.

The marriage of these two clever, gifted and beautiful people looked to be made in heaven. The early years were tough, however, with Jackie suffering first a miscarriage and then a stillbirth, before their daughter Caroline was born in 1957. Meanwhile, Jack was often ill and already indulging his notorious penchant for affairs.

When the White House beckoned, Jackie showed both her style and her steel. Though pregnant throughout the 1960

presidential campaign (John junior was born two weeks after the election), she hired a politically astute social secretary to advise her and regularly accompanied her husband on the campaign trail. Shocked by the rundown state of the presidential residence, she determined to make it both a comfortable family home and a showcase for American history and talent. Initially drawing criticism at the cost, this move came to be understood as a brilliant statement of a new era. In February 1962, Jackie led a nationally televised tour of the White House and it became a new and regular venue for cultural performances by US companies.

Jackie was concerned, at the same time, to guard the privacy of her children and appeared infrequently in public, though making a point of getting it right when she did. In her pillbox hats, Chanel suits and elegantly comfortable flat shoes, she influenced a generation of women. When the Kennedys visited France in 1962, she

charmed the French with her style, ease of manner and command of their language – JFK ruefully described himself as 'the man who accompanied Jacqueline Kennedy to France.'

The year of JFK's death had already been a tragic one for the couple, as their son, Patrick, died two days after his birth in August. After the bleak November day in Dallas, when her husband was killed, Jackie impressed the world with her stoicism, dignity and courage.

Her marriage to the Greek shipping magnate, Aristotle Onassis, in 1968, was less popular, but the assassination of Robert Kennedy six months earlier had left Jackie in fear for her children's safety and she wanted them out of the US. After Onassis' death in 1975, Jackie reinvented herself yet again, as a writer, editor and publisher, while continuing to work to preserve and protect America's cultural heritage.

Right: After the traumatic events of 1963, Jacqueline Kennedy demonstrated purposeful survival instincts. In 1975 she returned to New York for a successful publishing career.

Left: Graceful, elegant and beautiful, Kennedy was widely praised for her dignity in the wake of her husband's assassination.

Dolly Parton

Born Dolly Rebecca Parton
January 19, 1946
Sevierville, Tennessee,
USA

Blessed with a distinctive soprano and a deceptively 'dumb blonde' appearance, the 'Queen of Country Music' is one of the most successful female country music singers. She has had a record-breaking number of hits over her 50-year career.

The fourth of 12 children, Dolly Parton was raised in a one-room cabin in rural Tennessee, with music a fundamental part of her upbringing. As a child, she learned to play guitar and banjo and began to make up songs. Appearing regularly on a local radio variety show, she made her debut at the Grand Ole Opry in Nashville in 1958, aged 13. She moved to Nashville for good in 1964 and her first hit single was *Dumb Blonde*, which attracted the attention of country star, Porter Wagoner. He invited her to join his weekly syndicated television program and they made an almost uninterrupted string of Top Ten singles together over the next six years.

Initially, Parton's solo efforts were less successful, but in 1970 *Joshua* finally made it to the No. 1 slot, followed closely by *Coat of Many Colors* (1971), which described her poverty-stricken childhood and swiftly became her signature tune and finally, *Jolene* (1974). That was also the year that she finally left Wagoner's show, writing the classic *I Will Always Love You* to commemorate the relationship. It was a measure of her business savvy that she refused Elvis Presley's request to cover the song, because it would have meant signing away half the rights. The song has made her millions and she earned the admiring title 'the Iron Butterfly.' Between 1974 and 1980, she had eight more No. 1 hits, winning a Grammy in 1977 for Best Female Country Vocal Performer.

Parton's big screen debut was in 1980, when she played a brassy Southerner in *Nine to Five,* opposite Jane Fonda and Lily Tomlin and won an Oscar nomination for the title song. Many more films have followed, including *Rhinestone* (1984), in which she sang a duet with Sylvestor Stallone and the star-studded *Steel Magnolias* (1989). In 1986, she established Dolly Parton Enterprises to control her growing empire and also began to support a number of charities, notably a drive to improve literacy, by distributing free books.

Meanwhile, the string of hit singles continued, with five No.1 solo hits between 1981 and 1984, plus her duet with Kenny Rogers, *Islands in the Stream.* Country fans were becoming critical of this more mainstream focus, but her album *Trio* (1987), with Linda Ronstadt and Emmylou Harris, re-established her as a true country singer and produced three Top Ten country singles.

The hit singles may have ended, but Parton's activities show no sign of slowing down. She published her autobiography in 1994, made another album with Ronstadt and Harris in 1999 and in 2008, released her first mainstream country album for 20 years, *Backwoods Barbie.*

Left: Dolly appeared with Porter Wagoner on his popular TV show from 1967 to 1974.

Right: Dolly admits she has had cosmetic surgery to maintain her voluptuous image.

The Rolling Stones

The Stones are one of the few groups from the vibrant 1960s, who are still going strong – despite changes in line-up – and performing as raunchily and successfully as ever, after nearly 50 years.

Founder members and boyhood friends Mick Jagger and Keith Richards got together in 1960 to share a taste for American R&B and to form their first band.

They soon met guitarist, Brian Jones and on July 12, 1962, played their first gig as the Rolling Stones, featuring Jagger, Richards and Jones, with bassist Dick Taylor, keyboardist Ian Stewart and Tony Chapman on drums. Bill Wyman soon replaced Taylor and in January 1963 drummer Charlie Watts was persuaded to give up his job in advertising to join the line-up.

The band's successful season in spring 1963, at a west London club attracted ex-Beatles publicist Andrew Loog Oldham, on the lookout for a competitor to The Beatles' clean-cut image. Their first singles were cover versions and they finally had a UK No. 1 with *It's All Over Now* in June 1964. What established the band, however, was their emphasis on black American blues and R&B – much

influenced by the music of Chuck Berry and Muddy Waters – in contrast to the Mersey Sound of The Beatles. They were also renowned for their sensational, drug-fueled live performances, which brought them shocked press coverage. Their US tour, in June 1964, was a huge success, with riots in Chicago; their version of the blues standard *Little Red Rooster*, a UK No. 1, was banned in the US for its 'objectionable' lyrics.

In the mid-1960s, Oldham encouraged Jagger and Richards to begin writing their own numbers, which led to a string of pioneering, sophisticated and ironic singles – *The Last Time*, *(I Can't Get No) Satisfaction*, *Get Off My Cloud*, *19th Nervous Breakdown* and *Mother's Little Helper*. In January 1967, the Stones caused a sensation when they performed *Let's Spend the Night Together* on the *Ed Sullivan Show* – with Jagger mumbling

the lines after threats of censorship. The bad-boy image was reinforced later that year, by the arrest in the UK of Jagger, Richards and Jones on drugs possession charges and the death of Brian Jones from a drug overdose, in summer 1969.

In the 1970s, the band seemed, for a while, to lose direction, but their three-yearly US tours were all sell-outs. In 1976, Ronnie Wood became Jones's replacement. Jagger and Richards fell out in the 1980s and there was a recording lull, while bassist Bill Wyman quit in 1992. But although the Stones' album sales generally slowed, the band was and continues to be, a sell-out on tour. Their 'Bigger Bang' tour, which ran for two years from 2005, was the highest grossing tour of all time and even took in the 2006 Super Bowl. It was immortalized by film-maker Martin Scorsese *in Shine a Light* (2008).

Founded	1962
Founder members:	Mick Jagger, Keith Richards, Brian Jones, Dick Taylor, Ian Stewart, Tony Chapman
Current members:	Mick Jagger, Keith Richards, Ronnie Wood, Charlie Watts

Left: The Stones in their heyday, New York, 1964. From left, Jagger, Jones, Wyman, RIchards and Watts.

Below: The Stones during the 2006 Superbowl.

Overleaf: Jagger's performances remain as lively as ever.

Diana Ross

Born Diana Ernestine Earle Ross
March 26, 1944
Detroit, Michigan, USA

American singer and actress, Diana Ross, was the most successful female vocalist of the rock era. She played a crucial role in the creation of the 1960s Motown Sound, as lead singer of the female vocal group, the Supremes and went on to launch a hugely successful solo career.

Like many of her contemporaries, Ross learned to sing and harmonize in her local Baptist church choir. She was soon singing with Florence Ballard and Mary Wilson in a girls' vocal group, the Primettes. The time was ripe: Berry Gordy founded the first African-American-owned labels, Tamla Records in 1959 and Motown Records in 1960, in Ross's home town of Detroit. By the time the Primettes auditioned for the label in 1962, Motown was on the way to becoming a major force in the music industry, with its pop-influenced soul sound.

Gordy recognized the group's cross-over potential, signing them up and changing their name to the Supremes. Initially, they worked as a backing group for solo artists, such as Marvin Gaye and Mary Wells. Their first eight singles went nowhere and it was August 1964, before they had the first of five successive No. 1 hits with *Where Did Our Love Go*. The hits that followed, including *Baby Love*, made the group the most successful in the US in the 1960s, and they were only outstripped globally by The Beatles.

From an early stage, Gordy saw Ross, with her alluring stage presence and soaring, well-trained voice, as a potential solo performer and Ross had the ambition to match. Following Ballard's departure in 1967, the group began to be marketed as Diana Ross and the Supremes. Then, in 1969, Ross embarked on her solo career with the album *Diana Ross* and her first hit single *Ain't No Mountain High Enough*. The following year, *I'm Still Waiting* became her first UK No. 1.

A string of television appearances was followed by her acclaimed role in *Lady Sings the Blues* (1972), a biopic of jazz icon Billie Holliday. Ross's casting was initially ridiculed, on the grounds that her persona and singing style were very different from Holliday's. But she immersed herself in the music and won universally favorable reviews and even an Oscar nomination. Several more film roles followed, including *Mahogany* (1975) and the loss-making *The Wiz* (1978).

The 1980s saw a change of record label, with Ross moving to MCA and scoring a hit with *Muscles* (1982), written by her friend and protégé, Michael Jackson. Though sales faltered in the 1980s and 1990s, she continued to make regular television appearances. A planned Supremes tour in 2000 was much criticized for failing to include founder member Mary Wilson and was eventually canceled. The recordings continued, however, with an album of love songs in 2006, *I Love You*. In 2007, Ross's achievements were recognized with a John F. Kennedy Center for the Performing Arts Honors Award.

Left: Diana Ross and the Supremes (left, Florence Ballard, center, Mary Wilson), 1965.

Below: Ross wears a flamboyant headdress during a 2004 concert in Rotterdam, the Netherlands.

Michael Schumacher

German racing driver, Michael Schumacher ('Schumi' or 'Schuey'), has won the Formula One World Championship a record-breaking seven times. He also holds the Formula One records for most race victories, most wins in a season, most career pole positions, most points in a season and most consecutive World Championships – five between 2000 and 2004.

The young Michael showed his racing passion early and was introduced to karting by his parents, winning his first club championship aged only six and swiftly attracting sponsorship from local businessmen. Unable to get a karting license in Germany until he was 14, he obtained one in Luxembourg at the age of 12 and won the German Junior Kart championship in 1982. Leaving school to become a mechanic, he took his first step into single-seat car racing in 1988, winning the German Formula König series. In 1990, he won the German Formula Three championship and was hired by Mercedes to drive sports cars.

He won his first Formula One race for them in 1992, going on to win another 18 races and two World Championships in his next four seasons. His first championship, in 1994, was marred by claims of technical irregularities and a debatable collision, but Schumacher came back strongly in 1995, to take the title with ease, becoming the youngest ever driver to win the championship twice.

Joining Ferrari for the 1996 season, he began promisingly, with three wins in 1996 and five in 1997, while in 1998, he finished second overall. The serious record breaking began in 2000, when Schumacher became Ferrari's first world champion in 21 years. He went on to win the title for four more successive seasons, the last in 2004, by a massive margin, having won 13 out of the season's 18 races. Announcing his retirement at the end of the 2006 season, he finished with yet more records, scoring seven more victories, to bring his career total to 91 (40 more than his nearest rival).

Born January 3, 1969
Hürth-Hermülheim, near Cologne, Germany

Throughout his career, Schumacher has been noted for his ability to produce fast laps at the crucial moment, to get the maximum out of his car, while understanding its limits and to make the most of difficult wet conditions, earning him the title *Regenmeister* (rain master). He is widely acknowledged to be the world's best ever racing driver.

On his retirement from racing driving, Schumacher became a consultant to Ferrari, lending his expertise for both car and team development. A planned comeback, in 2009, had to be canceled, after a motor bike crash, but he signed a three-year contract with the Mercedes GP Petronas team in 2009 and returned to Formula One racing in the 2010 season.

Schumacher's Formula One debut was impressive – he qualified seventh for the 1991 Belgian Grand Prix at Spa and was immediately signed by Benetton-Ford.

Right: Schumacher celebrates his win in the Belgian Grand Prix, 1995. Statistically, he is the most successful Formula One driver ever.

Below: Driving for the Ferrari team during the 1997 Spanish Grand Prix.

Arnold Schwarzenegger

Former bodybuilder, Arnold Schwarzenegger, has made a long journey from an Austrian village, first to Hollywood acting glory and then to political power. He is currently serving a second term as the 38th governor of the state of California.

Beginning his bodybuilding career in his early teens, Schwarzenegger won the Junior Mr Europe title in 1965. The following year, he made his first plane trip to take part in the Mr Universe contest in London. Staying on to train with one of the judges, he became the youngest person ever to win the title in 1967.

Schwarzenegger was determined from an early age to get to the US, the land of opportunity. He moved to California in 1968, despite his still basic English and trained at Gold's Gym in Santa Monica. In 1970, he won the Mr Olympia title, the highest accolade in international professional bodybuilding and went on to win it again for five consecutive years, before announcing his retirement in 1975.

Meanwhile he had been working hard to break into films, ignoring discouraging feedback about his unusual appearance and heavy accent. He was Hercules in the dire *Hercules in New York* (1969), where his voice was dubbed to make him comprehensible and then played a deaf-mute in Altman's *The Long Goodbye* (1973), before taking a more substantial role with Jeff Bridges in *Stay Hungry* (1976). The documentary *Pumping Iron* (1976), about the 1975 Mr Olympia competition, first brought Arnie to public attention. But his major breakthrough came with the violent and successful *Conan the Barbarian* (1982), which met

a huge demand for live action movies in the 1980s and led to a host of similar roles. Movies such as *Twins* (1988), with Danny de Vito, demonstrated that Schwarzenegger was not a one-trick wonder and could really act.

Superstardom was assured by what will undoubtedly remain Schwarzenegger's signature part, as the titular character in *The Terminator*, James Cameron's 1984 sci-fi epic and its two sequels. He brought an element of self-deprecating humor and even pathos to what was otherwise an all-action role. *Terminator 2: Judgment Day* was the highest grossing film of 1991 and Schwarzenegger was named International Star of the Decade in 1993.

Schwarzenegger married into American political aristocracy in 1986, when he wed television journalist Maria Shriver, daughter of John F. Kennedy's sister, Eunice. He himself has long been a Republican supporter and accompanied Ronald Reagan's Vice-President, George

Bush, on the presidential campaign in 1988. In 2003, he announced his intention to run for the governorship of California and defeated a crowded field of candidates; he was reelected by a substantial majority in 2006. The astute and adaptable Schwarzenegger has proved a relatively moderate and popular governor, making a commitment to tackle global warming and signing into law in 2007, the state's first cap on greenhouse emissions.

Born Arnold Alois Schwarzenegger July 30, 1947 Thal, Graz, Austria

Left: Arnie in his most celebrated role, *The Terminator*, 1984.

Below: Elected governor of California in 2003, Schwarzenegger is sometimes nicknamed 'the Governator' in tribute to his most famous role.

The Simpsons

Matt Groening's animated show
The Simpsons – starring a crazy, but
lovable yellow-skinned family – has
become the longest-running sitcom in
television history. It gave a satirical edge
to primetime television in the early 1990s
and was a major factor in establishing
newcomer, Fox, as a legitimate
broadcasting television network.

The series was conceived when cartoonist
Groening was invited to pitch ideas for
animation shorts to producer James L.
Brooks for *The Tracey Ullman Show*.
Initially, Brooks wanted him to adapt the
characters from his *Life in Hell* cartoon,
but Groening was reluctant to jeopardize
his ownership rights and instead came
up with the idea of a dysfunctional
family. The characters first appeared
on *The Tracey Ullman Show* on
April 19, 1987. Groening submitted
basic sketches to the animators,
assuming they would be tidied up,
but the animators simply retraced
his drawings. It was George Peluse,

Created April, 1987

the colorist, who decided to make the characters yellow.

When Brooks negotiated a contract with Fox for a half-hour series called *The Simpsons*, he stipulated the inclusion of a clause preventing Fox from interfering with content. Groening's stated intention was to offer an alternative to 'mainstream trash'. The show is notable not only for its wide-ranging cultural references – which typically include Susan Sontag, Ayn Rand and *The Bridges of Madison County* in a single episode – but also for its raw parodying of the hypocrisies and contradictions found within society. So, dimwit patriarch, Homer, tells bright daughter, Lisa, that it is all right to steal 'from people you don't like' and the Reverend Lovejoy lies to win an argument. Behind them all looms the nuclear power plant, where the lazy and careless Homer works as a safety inspector.

The series premiered on December 17, 1989 and was the first Fox program to

gain a place in a season's Top 30 shows. In most episodes of the first three series, Bart – the delinquent oldest Simpson child – was the lead character. The series has sparked a huge amount of merchandizing: Bart T-shirts have sold millions, helped rather than hindered by the banning in some American schools of T-shirts with slogans, such as 'Underachiever (and proud of it!)'.

Early critical reception was ecstatic and the show spawned a whole series of copycat animations, such as the raucous *South Park. The Simpsons* has won numerous honors and awards: in 1998, *Time* magazine named it the 20th century's best television series, while in 2008, it was first on *Entertainment Weekly*'s list of Top 100 shows of the past 25 years. It has notched up a total of 25 Primetime Emmy Awards.

Latterly, there have been some suggestions that it is running out of steam – a charge vigorously denied by Groening. Certainly the spin-offs continue: *The Simpsons Movie* (2007) was both critically and financially a winner. The show's 20th anniversary season in 2009–10 was celebrated by Morgan Spurlock's documentary, *The Simpsons 20th Anniversary Special! In 3–D! On Ice!*, which was shown alongside the 450th episode to celebrate 'the cultural phenomenon of *The Simpsons*'.

Above: Cartoonist and Simpsons' creator Matt Groening poses with the world's favorite yellow family, 1990.

Left: Homer's famous exasperated 'D'oh' is now so well-known that it is listed in the *Oxford English Dictionary*.

Frank Sinatra

Born Francis Albert Sinatra
December 12, 1915
Hoboken, New Jersey,
USA

Died May 14, 1998
Los Angeles, California,
USA

The classic rags-to-riches story of Frank Sinatra, superstar singer and Oscar-winning actor, encapsulates all that is most appealing about 20th-century America. His many nicknames – 'Ol' Blue Eyes', 'The Chairman of the Board' and simply 'The Voice', to name just a few – give some idea of the adulation and respect he commanded.

The only child of Italian immigrants, Sinatra decided early on that he wanted to be a singer. His career began in the big-band 'swing' era: he signed with the Tommy Dorsey Orchestra in 1940, when he first attracted the adulation of teenage fans, the so-called bobbysoxers.

Launching a solo career in 1942, he began a four-week slot on Benny Goodman's post-Christmas show at the New York Paramount on December 30 – and a legend was born. *Variety* hailed him as the 'hottest thing in show-biz' and his live appearances continued to charm audiences worldwide to the end of his career. A contract with Columbia and a series of concerts with four of American's leading orchestras followed in 1943. With his frail and vulnerable image (he was turned down for war service on health grounds), naturally tuneful voice and well-honed technique, he brought passion and feeling back to singing.

Films soon beckoned and in 1945, Sinatra made *Anchors Aweigh* with Gene Kelly, which led to a five-year contract with MGM. The late 1940s saw a slide in his recording career, problems at MGM and a tempestuous on-off relationship with Ava Gardner, that ended his first marriage. But the classic war movie *From Here to Eternity* (1953), Sinatra's first non-singing role,

finally proved that he was an actor as well as a crooner: it won him an Oscar for Best Supporting Actor and relaunched his film career. A string of successful roles followed – a psychopathic assassin in *Suddenly* (1954), the feckless Nathan Detroit in *Guys and Dolls* (1955) with Marlon Brando, a reformed junkie in *The Man with the Golden Arm* (1955) and a hopeful journalist in *High Society* (1956), with Grace Kelly and Bing Crosby.

From the late 1950s, Sinatra launched into the album market and focused on a more adult audience, now that rock was taking over the hit parade. *Songs for Swingin' Lovers!* (1956), a subtle big band album, including all-time favorites such as *I've Got You Under My Skin* and *You Make Me Feel So Young*, was an early high point. He also turned successful businessman, buying his way into legalized gambling in Nevada and establishing his own hugely successful record label, Reprise, in 1960. A brief retirement (1971–3) ended with another

flow of recordings and sell-out live appearances. Frank Sinatra's 75th birthday tour in 1990 was a critical triumph and in 1995, to mark his 80th birthday, the Empire State Building glowed blue.

Right: Ol' Blue Eyes in 1954 at the height of his fame.

Below: Sinatra retired in 1971, but returned to recording just two years later and by the early 1980s, had revived his popularity.

Overleaf: Frank Sinatra (right) pictured with Grace Kelly and Bing Crosby, his fellow stars in the 1956 movie *High Society*.

Howard Stern

Born Howard Allan Stern
January 12, 1954
Queens, New York City,
USA

American 'shock jock', Howard Stern, the highest paid radio personality in the US, came to national prominence in the 1990s, with his explicit and provocative morning radio show.

A bright child and an early radio fan, Stern was attracted to Boston University in 1972, because of its reputation in broadcast communications and graduated magna cum laude in 1976. His early experience was at rock radio stations in New York, Hartford and Detroit, followed by the station DC-101 in Washington DC, where he more than tripled his audience in little over a year, with his mix of music and playful phone calls. In 1982, he signed a five-year deal with NBC for the afternoon program on their flagship WNBC station in New York City. Already, some of Stern's comic material had upset listeners, however and NBC monitored his show intensely. At first, Stern played ball, but gradually he introduced slots, such as 'Sexual Innuendo Wednesday' and 'Mystery Whiz' and in 1985, he was fired.

It was at New York City's WXRK station, better known as K-ROCK, that Stern really got going. Establishing his own on-air team and provocatively confronting touchy subjects that others preferred to avoid – like race, sex and death – he soon earned top ratings on his morning program, where he stayed for nearly 20 years. In 1986, he syndicated his show, allowing him to break into other US markets – first Philadelphia and Washington DC and ultimately, Los Angeles, New Orleans, Boston and Dallas. In 1992, he was the first to top New York and Los Angeles ratings simultaneously, by 1993, he was claiming 3 million daily listeners and by 1995, he was reportedly earning $8 million a year.

His autobiography, characteristically called *Private Parts*, hit the bestseller list in 1993 and stayed there for a month, proving the fastest selling title in its publisher's history.

The outrageousness continued, with Stern causing deep offence, by his would-be humorous comments on the murder of the Mexican American singer Selena in 1995 and on the Columbine High School shootings in 1999. By 2004 his employers had been fined some $2.5 million in total by the Federal Communications Commission, for breaches of the broadcasting code and he was dropped by the US media giant Clear Channel.

It was at this point that Stern changed the face of American radio by quitting the public airwaves. Instead, he signed a five-year $500 million contract with the unregulated subscription satellite network, Sirius, saying 'I left because I couldn't stand the censorship.' His move helped catapult satellite radio to public awareness. When he announced his move, Sirius had 650,000 listeners. In 2005, it added 2.2 million new subscribers and by the end of 2008, could boast more than 19 million.

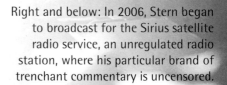

Right and below: In 2006, Stern began to broadcast for the Sirius satellite radio service, an unregulated radio station, where his particular brand of trenchant commentary is uncensored.

U2

Founded 1976

Members Bono (Paul Hewson)
The Edge (David Evans)
Adam Clayton
Larry Mullen Jr.

Irish rock band U2 are one of the supergroups of the age, a politically conscious band whose music fills stadiums with diehard fans around the globe. They are one of the most commercially successful bands in the world, having sold more than 150 million records and won 22 Grammy awards.

Founded in Dublin in 1976 by 14-year-old drummer Larry Mullen Jr., U2 began life as Feedback and changed their name to The Hype, before settling on U2. Influenced by punk, in 1978, they won a talent show in Limerick, with the prize of recording a demo for CBS Ireland and by 1980, they had released two moderately successful records in Ireland.

With their signing to Island Records and the release of their first album, *Boy*, in 1980, U2's fortunes took off. Bono's earnest lyrics, complemented by the band's dynamic playing, made for formidable live performances and the band consolidated their position as a serious rock band, with the release, in 1983, of the chart-topping album *War*. It included the single *Sunday Bloody Sunday* – a powerful response to the conflict in Northern Ireland – and *New Year's Day*, which reached No. 10 in the UK chart.

The band began a fruitful collaboration in 1984 with producer Brian Eno, who added a new ambient direction and rich orchestral sound to their output on

The Unforgettable Fire (1984). *Pride (In the Name of Love)*, a tribute to Martin Luther King, was their first American hit single. They moved on from this experimentation to embrace the folk and blues roots of American rock on their 1987 album *The Joshua Tree*. The fastest selling album in British chart history, it remained at No. 1 for nine weeks in the US.

Achtung Baby (1991) continued the band's reputation for reinvention, with their music taking on a new feel inspired by dance music. Their live performances on the 'Zoo TV' tour of 1992–3 assumed an extravagant multimedia guise. In their postmodern way, they embraced the excesses of the world of cable TV and satellite news, in order to satirize it and continued to poke fun at commercialism, with their 1997 'Popmart' tour. *All That You Can't Leave Behind* (2000) was classic U2, with an accomplished sound and produced two exceptional singles, *Beautiful Day* and *Stuck in a Moment You Can't Get Out Of*, which supplied two of the album's seven Grammy awards.

Away from the music, U2 have worked to address the world's problems of social injustice and disease and Bono in particular, has concerned himself with global issues of poverty and debt in the developing world. The band continue to tour and make albums, cementing their status as one of the iconic rock acts of recent times.

Left: U2, during the Joshua Tree Tour, 1987. From left to right – Larry Mullen, Jr., The Edge, Bono and Adam Clayton.

Below: Bono performs *In the Name of Love* during the We Are One: Inaugural Celebration at the Lincoln Memorial in Washington to celebrate the presidential inauguration of Barack Obama, 2009.

Andy Warhol

Born Andrew Warhola
August 6, 1928
Pittsburgh, Pennsylvania,
USA

Died February 22, 1987
New York City, USA

Famous for saying that 'In the future everyone will be famous for 15 minutes', Andy Warhol himself found fame as an innovative artist that lasted much longer. One of the prime movers behind the Pop Art movement of the 1960s, he was an influential and iconoclastic graphic artist and film-maker.

Born in Pittsburgh, Pennsylvania to Slovak immigrants, Warhol studied commercial art at the Carnegie Institute of Technology in Pittsburgh, before moving to New York, in 1949, to work in magazine illustration and advertising. He also began to design album covers in the wake of the rapid expansion of the recording industry at the end of the 1950s and in 1957, his shoe advertisements won an award.

His first solo exhibition, in Los Angeles in November 1962, is regarded as a revolutionary moment in art, when his careful depictions of everyday objects in oils turned art on its head. He embraced the commercialization of society, using mass advertising as the basis for his work and became one of the leading exponents of Pop Art. He drew on iconic American products and people for his inspiration and his first exhibition included the *Marilyn Diptych* (containing 50 images of Marilyn Monroe), *100 Soup Cans* and *100 Coke Bottles*.

Warhol did not believe in the veneration of art for art's sake, or that fine art should be produced just for rich connoisseurs. He used the silk screen process to ensure that his works could be reproduced again and again and remarked that 'America started the tradition where the richest consumers buy essentially the same things as the poorest.' Though he was referring to Coca Cola, this belief extended to his art. He used assistants and collaborators to produce his works, manufacturing the silk screens in his infamous 'Factory' in New York. A meeting place for artists and bohemian hangers-on, it was also the scene of extravagant parties.

In 1965, Warhol announced his retirement from art, in order to concentrate on film-making and music. He became the manager of the Velvet Underground rock group and designed their first album cover, *The Velvet Underground and Nico*, in 1967. He directed more than 60 movies, all avant-garde and experimental works, that challenged the viewer. His earliest films, such as *Sleep* (showing a man sleeping for six hours), were silent and almost entirely static, but after Warhol was shot by one of his actors in 1968, he surrendered more control to his assistant, Paul Morrissey. Movies such as *Chelsea Girls*, *Flesh* and *Trash* attracted a wider audience.

Increasingly reclusive, Warhol maintained a remote public face, but remained a cult figure in the New York art scene during the 1970s and 1980s. Since his death, in 1987, his works have continued to command high prices and in 1994, the Warhol Museum opened in his home town of Pittsburgh.

Left and below: Avant-garde and iconoclastic, Warhol and his work were always interesting and provocative.

Shane Warne

The foremost Australian cricketer of his generation, Shane Warne is regarded as one of the finest bowlers in the history of the game. His fearsome legbreak googly bowling has confounded some of the best international cricketers and forced many batsmen to rethink their game.

Warne began his cricket career as a schoolboy, graduating to the University of Melbourne Cricket Club in 1983. His early skill earmarked him for future glory and he was selected to train at the Australian Cricket Academy in Adelaide. His Test match debut, in January 1992, against India, was disappointing. But 18 months later, he established what became his trademark style, when he bowled English veteran Mike Gatting out with the opening ball of a Test match at Old Trafford, Manchester. A piercingly accurate wrist-spinner, Warne's ball became known as the 'Ball of the Century' and was as astonishing, as it was dramatic, seeing off one of England's finest batsmen.

Warne had grown up watching the dominance of international fast bowlers, but he almost singlehandedly revived the leg spin, a tricky maneuver which had almost died out, because it is so difficult to execute successfully. Batsman feared Warne – who was nicknamed the 'Sultan of Spin' – enabling him to establish a psychological dominance that spooked many men, even before he had bowled them his first ball.

Warne's batting was as aggressive as his bowling – he scored over 3,000 Test runs – and he also proved to be a highly successful slip fielder with an uncanny ability to catch balls, but it is his bowling that has toppled records. In 2004, he became only the second cricketer to take 500 Test wickets and just over a year later, became the first player to take 600.

Warne retired from international cricket in 2007, but continued to play for Hampshire in English county cricket and latterly, for the Rajasthan Royals in the Indian Premier League. He is also a respected commentator. His cricketing accolades are impressive, from the Wisden Cricketer of the Year in 1994 to his selection as one of the five Wisden Cricketers of the Century in 2000, alongside Viv Richards, Jack Hobbs, Don Bradman and Gary Sobers.

In a game that distinguishes between gentlemen and players, Warne is definitely among the latter. Ferociously competitive, he is a larger-than-life figure, whose career has seen its fair share of controversy – he was banned for a year in 2003, for failing a drugs test.

Born	Shane Keith Warne
	September 13, 1969
	Upper Ferntree Gully,
	Victoria, Australia

His flamboyant personality meant that he was never elevated to captain the Australian Test side. This was a shame, because when he captained the Australian side in one-day internationals, he proved to be an inspiring leader, taking the team to ten victories out of 11 matches. Putting his shortcomings aside, many commentators agree that he is one of cricket's great icons.

Right: Warne celebrates his 700th test wicket, 2006.

Below: Warne was the unassailable colossus of Australian cricket in the 1990s and early years of the 21st century.

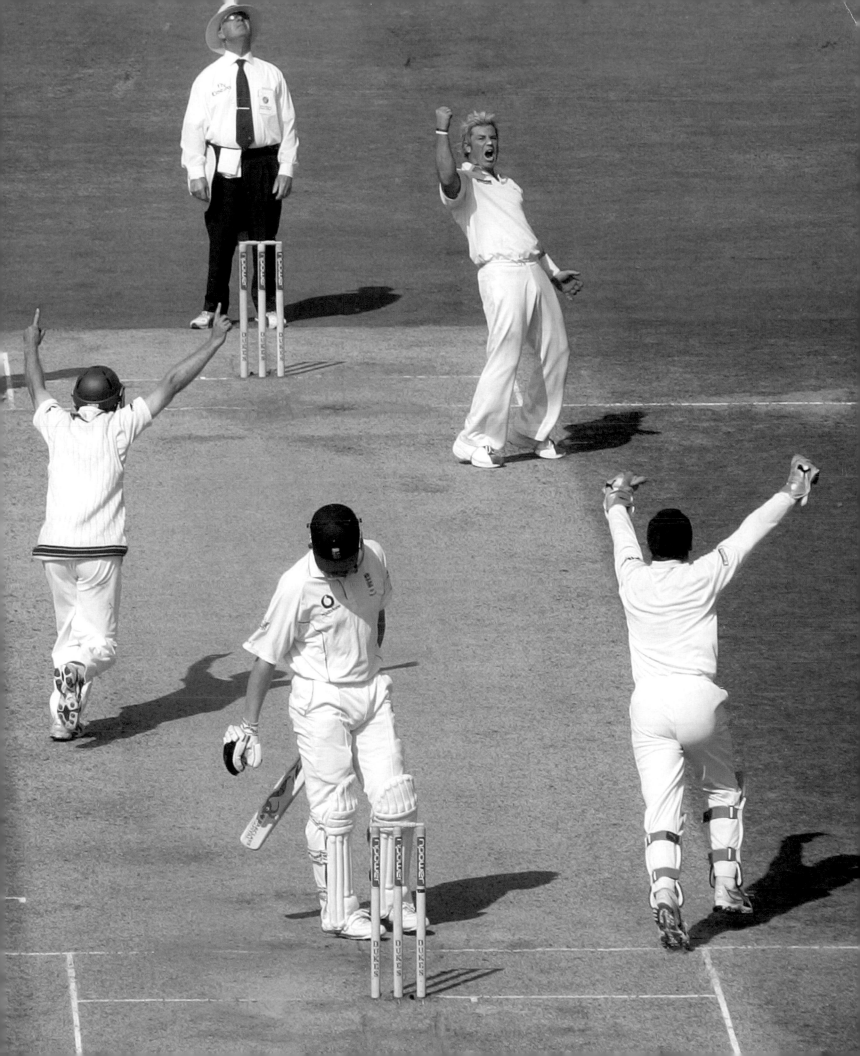

Dame Vivienne Westwood

Vivienne Westwood is one of Britain's most talented fashion designers. Her eye-catching clothes are imaginative, refreshing and often outrageous; her impact on the world of fashion cannot be underestimated. One of the founders of the punk rock, her signature style is to combine classic tailoring with unconventional additions to produce strikingly original designs.

Born in the north of England, Westwood moved to London with her family when she was 17 and studied at the Harrow School of Art. Ever practical, she left after a short time because she simply could not see how art would support her financially. Instead, she became a schoolteacher and in her spare time made jewelry. She married Derek Westwood, had a son and lived a fairly conventional life until she met Malcolm McLaren in 1965, a man as creative and anti-establishment as herself. They started a relationship and had a son and a working partnership that lasted from 1970 until 1984, opening a shop called *Let It Rock* in 1971.

Their shop underwent frequent changes of name and identity: as *Sex* in 1975 it sold fetish gear and rubber; as *Seditionaries – Clothes for Heroes* from 1976, the emphasis was on subversive fashion. Vivienne's designs of ripped 1950s gear, tartan trousers bedecked with chains, leather, and buckles were popular, expensive and controversial. Her clothes were at the heart of the punk movement, which McLaren initially masterminded, and were copied throughout the world.

By the early 1980s Westwood wanted to devote all her time to fashion, believing 'you have a much better life if you wear impressive clothes'. The shop was renamed yet again, as *World's End*, and in 1981 Westwood launched her first full fashion collection, entitled 'Pirate'. She captured the national imagination with unisex clothes that fired up the New Romantic look of the era. She continued to collaborate with McLaren until 1984, when she traveled to Italy and Japan for new inspiration.

In 1989 Westwood launched her Harris Tweed designs, celebrating her love of classic tailoring and fine British fabrics, rendered with the customary Westwood twist. In the 1990s, subsequent collections repeated this pattern of using classic patterns, eclectic inspiration and humorous, even parodic reinterpretation. Her work incorporates historical references – such as corsets, bustiers and bustles – with practicality, imagination and innovation.

Westwood has relentlessly used her own historical and cultural researches to inspire her work. Although she has said, 'The only reason I'm in fashion is to destroy the word 'conformity'. Nothing's interesting to me unless it's got that element', she has been delighted by the recognition she has received from the British Establishment – she was made a dame for services to fashion in 2006. Unorthodox, provocative and hugely talented, Vivienne Westwood is undoubtedly the most exciting fashion designer to emerge from Britain for many years.

> **Born** Vivienne Isabel Swire
> April 8, 1941
> Tintwistle, Derbyshire, UK

Left: The diminutive designer, Vivienne Westwood, surrounded by her models at her prêt à porter collection, 1997.

Right: Westwood presents her spring-summer collection in Paris, 1996.

Oprah Winfrey

Born Orpah [sic] Gail Winfrey
January 29, 1954
Kosciusko, Mississippi, USA

One of only a handful of global celebrities to be universally known simply by her first name, Oprah is one of the most influential women in the world thanks mainly to her hugely successful television chat show The Oprah Winfrey Show. She has used her influence to champion good causes, notably tackling child abuse, and is enormously philanthropic, giving large sums of money to many charities. around the world

Born in grinding poverty in America's Deep South, Winfrey survived a grim, abusive childhood, somehow emerging as a hard-working, talented and creative individual. She began her broadcasting career in Nashville at the age of 17, first on local radio and then two years later as a reporter and news anchor on the local TV station. At the same time she studied performing arts at Tennessee State University.

Her friendly, chatty persona shone through the news bulletins and after two years co-hosting the news in Baltimore, she moved to Baltimore's People Are Talking chat show in 1978. It was her next job, as host of AM Chicago, that established Oprah as the doyenne of chat show hosts. She took AM Chicago from bottom of the ratings in January 1984, right to the top, with audience figures beating those of Donohue, then Chicago's most popular talk show. Just 18 months later, The Oprah WInfrey Show was born and was broadcast from coast to coast across the USA. It quickly won numerous awards, not to mention staggering audience figures. Fans were drawn by Oprah's warmth and her ability to tackle all subjects. Empathetic and curious, straight talking, humorous and intelligent, she has a gift for making her guests reveal secrets that would otherwise have remained hidden.

Just as her TV career took off, in 1985 Oprah also launched herself in Hollywood, appearing in The Color Purple, and winning an Academy Award nomination for Best Supporting Actress. She followed this in 1988 by producing and starring in Beloved, and prepared for her role as a former slave by being trussed and blindfolded. Fellow actors were impressed by her dedication and natural dramatic ability.

Oprah is a woman with purpose who makes things happen. Audiences and fans are inspired by her positive and moral outlook on life and relate their life experiences to hers. Oprah has worked hard for her extraordinary good fortune, remaining at the heart of her business empire, Harpo Productions, and becoming the first female African-American billionaire in 2003. She uses much of her wealth to help the less fortunate in both the USA and abroad, founding the Oprah Winfrey Leadership Academy for Girls in South Africa,to educate a new generation of young women.

Right: Oprah celebrates the second anniversary of Oxygen Media, the women's television network she helped to found in 2000.

Below: Oprah at work on The Oprah Winfrey Show, America's most successful chat show. With a heady mixture of celebrity chat, confessional interviews, self-help and cultural discussions, the show is incredibly influential.

Stevie Wonder

Born Stevland Hardaway Judkins
May 13, 1950
Saginaw, Michigan, USA

A star since the age of 13, when he had his first No. 1 hit, Stevie Wonder has proved to be one of the most enduring talents in the music business. The winner of 22 Grammy awards, he has been an innovative, influential and pioneering force in the world of popular music.

Blind from birth, Stevie showed exceptional musical talents from an early age, when he sang in his church choir and played harmonica and piano. He was introduced to the legendary Berry Gordy of Motown Records and was promoted as 'Little Stevie Wonder', releasing his first single, in 1961, at the age of 11. At 13, he became the youngest person to achieve a No. 1 (a record that still stands) with his third single, *Fingertips (Pt. 2)*, for which he sang and played bongos and harmonica. He went on to have a number of Top Ten hits in the 1960s, including *For Once in My Life* (1968), *My Cherie Amour* (1969) and *Yester-Me, Yester-You, Yesterday* (1969).

Having dropped the 'Little' in the mid-1960s, Stevie Wonder renegotiated his contract with Motown in 1971, capitalizing on his success to demand total artistic control. He had proved with the 1970 album *Signed, Sealed & Delivered* that he could handle every aspect of a recording studio, writing his own material, playing most of the instruments himself and acting as his own producer and arranger. Gradually drawing on more exotic influences, he incorporated African and Latin rhythms with gospel, jazz and R&B influences

on *Music of My Mind* (1972). He began to use synthesizers, which became a signature of his sound. His next album, *Talking Book*, featured two of his best-loved No. 1 singles, *Superstition* and *You Are the Sunshine of My Life*.

Wonder overcame a serious car crash in 1973 to resume concerts and recording and despite his relative youth, was acknowledged as an important influence on musicians, from Jeff Beck to Bob Marley. Many of his songs have been covered by bands, such as The Jacksons and he is respected throughout the industry as a major songwriter, performer and producer.

Wonder recorded more sporadically in the 1980s, but returned time and again to political and social themes, such as his plea for an international holiday in memory of Martin Luther King, *Happy Birthday* (1980). He performed with

countless other international stars – Elton John, Michael Jackson, Gladys Knight and Julio Iglesias among others – and in 1984, won an Oscar for Best Original Song for *I Just Called to Say I Love You* from the movie *The Woman in Red*.

Aside from his outstanding musical achievements, Wonder is well known for his extensive humanitarian works for anti-Apartheid, AIDS and children's charities. Held in affectionate respect and admiration by peers, critics and fans alike, Stevie Wonder is one of the pivotal figures in popular music.

Left: 'Little' Stevie Wonder playing the harmonica, early in his career, during the 1960s.

Below: Stevie Wonder performs at the 25th Victoires de la Musique ceremony, held at the Zenith in Paris, 2010.

Tiger Woods

Born Eldrick Tont Woods
December 30, 1975
Cypress, California, USA

Tiger Woods is one of the most successful professional golfers of all time. He has won 14 major golf championships and achieved more major career victories than any other current player.

Woods was a golfing prodigy, who showed tremendous talent when only a toddler and went on to win a number of amateur Junior World Golf Championships, encouraged by his father, Earl. He obtained a golf scholarship to Stanford University in 1994, but left in 1996 when he turned professional. He immediately displayed the qualities that have helped him throughout his career: determination, drive and astonishing talent.

In 1997, Woods shocked the golfing world by winning the Augusta Masters Tournament at the age of 21, the youngest player ever to do so and the first to win it at his first attempt. Since then, he has won three further Masters titles (in 2001, 2002 and 2005); the US Open (2000, 2002 and 2008); the British Open (2000, 2005 and 2006); and the PGA Championship (1999, 2000, 2006 and 2007). He has earned over $111 million in prize money, more than any other player and has more major championships to his name than any golfer, other than the legendary Jack Nicklaus. The only tournament in which he has failed to excel is the Ryder Cup, the biennial team effort of the golfing calendar. The list of his career achievements is long, but suffice to say, he has spent more weeks as the golfing No. 1 than any other player.

Despite his incredible victories, Woods remains, at heart, a cautious player. He was one of the first golfers to dedicate hours to physical training and he plays fewer tournaments than most of his contemporaries, focusing his efforts on preparing really well for the big games.

Until 2009, Woods seemed to be the epitome of the restrained, ice-cool athlete, totally dedicated to his sport, but a series of misjudgments in his personal life gave rise to intense media speculation and showed the world that he was, after all, human. He announced a break from competitive golf in December 2009. In a rare televised speech, he acknowledged that he owed much of his success to his upbringing as a Buddhist, which 'teaches me to stop following every impulse and to learn restraint. Obviously I lost track of what I was taught,' he said, ruefully,in 2010.

Nevertheless, Woods has achieved the impossible – making golf sexy. Aside from his extraordinary talent, he is the most photogenic and charismatic international golfer in a generation and TV viewing figures go up dramatically when he plays. One of the most famous athletes in the world, he has become a multimillionaire, not only through his prize money, but also from corporate endorsement and sponsorship, notably from Nike. His career seems likely to continue for some years to come.

Left: Dedicated and hard-working, Woods spends long hours practicing and training.

Below: Tiger Woods hits the ball down the fairway in 2003, at the Torrey Pines Golf Course. He won the tournament with a score of 272.

Credits

All pictures are courtesy of Corbis Images, with individual photographers and additional agencies credited below.

Front Cover: main image, Lori Stoll / Retna Ltd., inset images (top to bottom), Jon Hrusa/epa, Kurt Krieger, Robert Maass, Gary Fabiano/Pool, Jazz Archiv/ Vas/dpa, Dziekan/Retna Ltd. Front Flap: Cat's Collection Back Cover: Bettmann Back Flap: Victor Fraile

Front End Paper Sunset Boulevard

1, 2	Sunset Boulevard
6-7	Lynn Goldsmith
8, 9, 10	Bettmann
11	Jean-François Rault/Kipa
12	Jean-Marie Leroy/Sygma
13	Victor Lerena/epa
14	(L) Sunset Boulevard; (top) Geoffrey Clements
15	John Springer Collection
16	Andy Rain/epa
17	Hulton-Deutsch Collection
18	Bettmann
19	Denis Balibouse/Reuters
20-21	Bettmann
22	Hulton-Deutsch Collection
23	Michael Ochs Archives
24-25	Hulton-Deutsch
26	Bettmann
27	Gianni Ciaccia/Sygma
28	Darren Whiteside/Reuters
29	Victor Fraile
30	Neal Preston
31	Corbis
32-35	James Palmer/Retna Ltd
36, 37	Sunset Boulevard
38, 39	Neal Preston
40	Bettmann
41	Hulton-Deutsch Collection
42	Sunset Boulevard
43	Bettmann
44	Neal Preston
45	Laura Levine
46, 47	Bettmann
48-9	Sunset Boulevard
50	Rune Hellestad
51	LAN
52	John Springer Collection
53	Steve Starr
54	Bob Penn/Sygma
55	Bill Ingalls/NASA Handout
56	Brooks Kraft
57	Soren Stache/epa
58	Marvin Koner
59	Marc Bryan-Brown
60, 61	Bettmann
62	John Springer Collection
63	Bettmann
64	Bettmann
65	Corbis
66	Steve Pope/epa
67	Roger Ressmeyer

68	Charles Peterson/Retna Ltd
69	Andy King/Sygma
70, 71	Sunset Boulevard
72	John Atashian
73	Jacques M. Chenet
74	Bettmann
75	Underwood & Underwood
76-7	John Bryson/Sygma
78-9	Bettmann
80	Lion's Gate Films/Bureau L.A. Collection
81, 82-3	Sunset Boulevard
84-5	Bettmann
86	Peter Andrews
87	Bureau L.A. Collection
88-9	Alessandra Benedetti
90	Douglas Kirkland
91	Photo B.D.V.
92	CinemaPhoto
93	Hulton-Deutsch Collection
94, 95	Bettmann
96	Bettmann
97	Sunset Boulevard
98	Michael Ochs Archives
99	Hulton-Deutsch Collection
100	Cat's Collection
101, 102-3	Sunset Boulevard
104	Underwood & Underwood
105	Bettmann
106	Pool Photograph/Corbis
107	Bettmann
108-9	Paul Hackett/Reuters
110-13	Sunset Boulevard
114	CinemaPhoto
115	Liz Hafalia/San Francisco Chronicle
116	Jim Bourg/Reuters
117	Tony Korody/Sygma
118	CinemaPhoto
119	Sunset Boulevard
120	Rune Hellestad
121	John A. Angelillo
122-3	Jared Milgrim
124, 125	Bettmann
126	CinemaPhoto
127	Douglas Kirkland
128	Doug Wilson
129	George Steinmetz
130	Corbis
131	Neal Preston
132	CinemaPhoto
133	Sunset Boulevard
134-5	Bettmann
136	Michael Nicholson
137	Swim Ink 2, LLC
138	Frank Trapper/Corbis Syma
139	Claudio Onorati/epa
140	Grant Smith
141	Rune Hellestad
142	Steffen Kugler/epa
143	Michael S. Yamashita
144	William James Warren/ Science Faction
145	Peter Tarnoff/Retna Ltd
146	Douglas Kirkland
147	Derek Hudson/Sygma (L); Sunset Boulevard

148, 149	Bettmann
150-1	John Springer Collection
152	Bettmann
153	Morton Beebe
154	CinemaPhoto
155	Sunset Boulevard
156	Michael Dalder
157	Henry Diltz
158-9	Bob KIng
160	Tomasso DeRosa
161	Frank Trapper
162	Robert Eric/Corbis Sygma
163	Michael Ochs Archives
164	Bettmann
165	Wally McNamee
166,167	John Springer Collection
168	René Maestri/Sygma
169	Bettmann
170-1	Sunset Boulevard
172	Ted Streshinsky
173, 174-5	Bettmann
176, 177	Bettmann
178	Hulton-Deutsch Collection
179	Henry Diltz
180-1	John Springer Collection
182	Hulton-Deutsch Collection
183	Sunset Boulevard
184	Frank Trapper
185	Stephane Cardinale/People Avenue
186	Gregory Pace
187	Andrew Marks
188	Simone Cecchetti
189	Neal Preston
190	Louise Gubb
191	STR New/Reuters
192-3	Gideon Mendel
194	Bernard Barbereau/Sygma
195	Robbie Jack
196	Jeff Albertson
197	Michael Ochs Archives
198	CinemaPhoto
199, 200-01	Sunset Boulevard
202	Alain Keler/Sygma
203	Denis O'Regan
204	Neal Preston
205	Neal Preston
206	Bettmann
207	John Springer Collection
208, 209	Pascal Della Zuana/Sygma
210	Daniel Deme/epa
211	Eric Robert/Corbis Sygma
212, 213, 214-5	Sunset Boulevard
216, 217	Henry Diltz
218	Bradley Smith
219, 220-1	Sunset Boulevard
222	Jason Reed/Reuters
223	Chuck Kennedy/Pool
224-5	Brooks Kraft
226	John Springer Collection
227, 228,-9	Bettmann
230	Henry Horenstein
231	Rob Brown
232	Claro Cortes IV/Reuters
233	Christian Charisius/Reuters
234	Bettmann
235	Reuters

236	Bettmann
237	Interpress/Interpress/Kipa
238, 239	Bettmann
240	Louie Psihoyos/Science Faction
241	Roger Ressmeyer
242	Richard Smith
243	Frank Trapper
244, 245	Michael Ochs Archives
246-7	Sunset Boulevard
248	Bettmann
249	Matt Campbell/epa
250-1	Lefranc David/Corbis KIPA
252	Michael Ochs Archives
253	RIck Nederstigt/epa
254	Jerome Prevost/TempSport
225	Philippe Eranian
256	CinemaPhoto
257	Robert Durrell/Reuters
258	Benoit Doppagne/epa
259	Richard Melloul/Sygma
260	Jay Dickman
261	Michael Ochs Archives
262-3	Gina James/Graylock/Retna
264-5	Close Murray/Corbis Sygma
266	Bettmann
267	Bernard Barbereau/Sygma
268-9	David Atlas/Retna Ltd.
270	Eckstein/Retna Ltd.
271	Alessandra Benedetti
272	Shannon Stapleton/Reuters
273	Ramin Talaie
274, 275	Cat's Collection
276	John Springer Collection
277	Bettmann
278	Cardniale Stephane/Corbis Sygma
279	Cortes/Retna Ltd.
280, 281, 282-3	Sunset Boulevard
284	Robert Maass
285	Kapoor Baldev/Sygma
286-7	Bettmann
288	Jean Guichard/Sygma
289	Richard Olivier
290	Neal Preston
291	Brooks Kraft
292	Victor Bockris
293	Karen Hardy/Sygma
294, 295	Philip Brown
296, 297	Photo B.D.V.
298	Martin Roe/Retna Ltd.
299	Gregory Pace
300	Bettmann
301	Stephane Cardinale/People Avenue
302, 303	Tony Roberts
Back End Paper	Bettmann

Project Managed by BlueRed Press Ltd